Rosemary Moon's
AGA
COOKBOOK

Rosemary Moon's

AGA
COOKBOOK

David & Charles

Colour artworks by Amanda Loverseed

ABOUT THE AUTHOR

Rosemary Moon first cooked on an Aga when staying with a schoolfriend, and after twenty years in the food business has finally achieved her ambition of owning one. A cookery writer and broadcaster known for no-nonsense but exciting dishes, she now brings her style of contemporary cuisine to the Aga. She lives in West Sussex.

Incidental line illustrations by Diana Knapp

AGA is a registered Trademark of Glynwed International plc.

A DAVID & CHARLES BOOK

First published in the UK in 1998
First published in the UK in paperback in 2001

ISBN 0 7153 1239 1

Typeset by ABM Typographics Ltd, Hull
Printed in China by Leefung-Asco Printers Ltd.
for David & Charles
Brunel House   Newton Abbot   Devon

These and other David & Charles books are available from all good bookshops. In case of difficulty, write to us at David & Charles *Direct,* PO Box 6, Newton Abbot, TQ12 2DW quoting reference M001, or call our credit card hotline on 01626 334555
Visit our website at www.davidandcharles.co.uk

Contents

Introduction

My love affair with Agas began when I aspired to a life on the road and a career in the orchestra pits and concert halls of the world – I wanted to be a trumpet player! I was staying with a girl-friend from the local Youth Orchestra in a house where a gleaming, blue oil-fired Aga had just been installed. I was hooked.

We girls had a wonderful weekend on our own, developing our culinary repertoire – I seem to remember a lemon meringue pie so large that we ended up eating it for lunch, supper and breakfast – and everything tasted utterly wonderful! Until my own Aga (two ovens, gas fired and claret-coloured – another passion!) was installed, that weekend had been my only real experience of Aga cookery, but it made a very deep and lasting impression. I swapped the concert platform for the kitchen long ago, but my dream of owning an Aga has only recently been fulfilled.

Once married and settled into our own cottage, how was I to convince my husband that an Aga was all we needed to complete our marital bliss? Well, it wasn't nearly as difficult as I had feared and was clinched by a weekend bread baking course. Nick has baked virtually all our bread since we married, and he is a perfectionist who would never consider using a machine for any part of the mixing or kneading. He produced the ultimate loaf in an electric fan oven and a gas cooker, but after a weekend with a master baker at the Village Bakery in Melmerby, was almost convinced that we needed a brick, wood-fired bread oven! However, as the baker had inferred that an Aga was the next best thing, operating on the same stored heat principle as a traditional brick oven, it was merely a matter of moments before I knew that thoughts of an Aga at home were no longer just a dream but a very real possibility.

The overwhelming image that accompanies an Aga is of rural, if not rustic, bliss. A casserole in the oven, gun dogs and chickens vying for space on the rug in front of it, and wellies and damp thornproofs steaming contentedly nearby. Although we do live in a 400 year-old cottage our lives are not nearly as divorced from the hubbub of civilisation as our most impractical fantasies would wish, so I know that you do not have to be miles from anywhere to truly appreciate an Aga.

Just as thornproofs are now considered suitable city wear, so around half of the Agas sold annually are installed in town or city properties. The profile of the Aga owner has changed, and is now finely balanced between the farming and country communities and the executive city dweller. The Aga owner of today is just as likely to be a gourmet who regularly eats out in bistros and top restaurants, as a skilled and passionate country cook who will have to travel thirty or forty miles to buy an aubergine or a jar of sun-dried tomatoes. Whereas the urban Aga owner may have easy access to all the ingredients needed to create Indian, Chinese, Italian and Pacific Rim dishes at home, the country cook may have to rely on mail order companies for the exotic, and the greenhouse or poly-tunnel for the designer salads which city-dwelling Brothers in Basting have simply to buy off the supermarket shelves, washed and mixed, ready to use in plastic bags.

This book has been written after two happy years with our Aga, and it is full of my favourite recipes – contemporary dishes such as you might eat in restaurants, see demonstrated on TV or read about regularly in cookbooks and magazines. The recipes show how to achieve stylish modern cuisine with your Aga, stretching the principles of cooking with stored heat to cope with the demands and techniques of contemporary cooking, whilst maximising the advantages of Aga cookery which are hard to imitate on a conventional domestic cooker.

Professional chefs turn their ranges on first thing in the morning and seldom switch them off again until after the last order at night. Because the oven is always on, they think nothing of roasting a fillet of salmon in a hot oven for 4–5 minutes, whereas the home cook would generally consider that to be unaccountably extravagant. Your Aga is on the whole time too, just waiting to be used, so such recipes can be completed without the slightest twinge of fiscal conscience. I have baked ciabattas on the floor of the Roasting Oven, achieving a crisp bottom crust and a light, soft crumb. I have mastered the arts of deep-frying and stir-frying, and can consistently create the crispest of pastry bases, which are much better than those produced on any of the other cookers that I have owned. The Aga may not have as many knobs and whistles as designer ranges and ovens, but who cares when it produces such excellent results?

COOKING WITH STORED HEAT

The Aga is thermostatically controlled to predetermined temperatures but, unlike other domestic cookers, it is on the whole time and is always ready to cook. According to proximity to the fire box, each area has a different temperature and is therefore used for a different style of cooking. Aga language does not, however, refer to exact temperatures but to a degree of heat and a style of cooking. Chefs talk about hot, medium and slow ovens but seldom refer to degrees Celsius or the gas regulo, and the Aga is just the same. The Roasting Oven could be called the Hot Oven, the Baking Oven on a four-oven Aga the Moderate Oven and the Simmering Oven is a perfect example of a Slow Oven, whilst the Warming Oven does just that, leaving the Simmering Oven free of plates and dishes for cooking. The hot plates are obvious – the Boiling Plate is fast whilst the Simmering Plate is slower. Four-oven Agas have an additional Warming Plate – a useful extension of the top of the Aga – for parking hot tins, warming extra dishes and resting meat before carving.

The heat indicator on the Aga is not so much a temperature monitor as an indicator of the amount of stored heat available. Things are just right when the mercury is on the thin black line. If it is in the red, your Aga is running too hot and the thermostat control needs adjusting, following the directions in your cooker instruction sheet. A lot of cooking will cause the indicator to drop as the heat is used up, and some cycling is normal in day-to-day running. If you have been doing a vast amount of cooking and the indicator is low, approaching the black, you will either have to wait for the heat to be restored, or allow longer for the food to cook. Don't keep adjusting the setting of your Aga – just keep an eye on it for two or three days after firing it up or having it serviced, get it just right and then leave it alone! Another good tip is to agree who is to tweak the control knob when the Aga is newly lit – yes, we both do it without communicating, resulting in nervous over-compensation.

The quickest way to lose heat from your Aga is to cook on the hot plates for an extended period of time. The chunky, porthole-like covers have to be that thick to retain the heat in the cooker, so if the covers are lifted, the heat can quickly escape. So much of our day-to-day cooking could be referred to as a Thirty Minute Fix, the type of dish that can be prepared and cooked from start to finish in half an hour or less. TV cooks frequently prepare quick and easy dishes that are very visual, often cooked totally on the hob since stir-frying and shallow frying are rapid and very visual. Although this is not an ideal method of cooking on the Aga – as much cooking as possible should be done in the ovens to conserve the heat – if you are simply using the Aga to prepare a quick supper, then there is no reason at all as to why you shouldn't cook in this way.

OTHER STORED HEAT COOKERS

The Aga name, like Hoover for vacuum cleaners, is synonymous with stored-heat cookers, but there are other similar ranges, some of which have variable temperature ovens. Although a specific temperature can be selected you should bear in mind that the response time on the ovens will not be as rapid as on a conventional oven, unless your range is fitted with an electric boost. If you wish to use my recipes for such an oven, I suggest you think of the Roasting Oven as about 220°C, the Baking Oven as 180°C and the Simmering Oven as 150°C, but do remember that all ovens will vary slightly in their settings. First get to know your cooker... start by trying some non-critical dishes such as those in the chapter on Slow Starts – Quick Finishes (page 64).

THE COLD SHELF

The heavy solid metal shelf supplied with the Aga is not really an extra large baking sheet. It is used to blank off extra heat, especially in the Roasting Oven, to create a cooler oven for more general cooking. You should always leave enough space between the food to be cooked and the shelf to allow a certain amount of heat to circulate – otherwise cooking will be uneven – and for some dishes, such as shortbread, you can transfer the shelf when hot from the Roasting Oven to the Simmering Oven to provide a hot surface that will ensure that the bases of critical dishes are cooked through as well as the tops.

The most important rule concerning the cold shelf is not to store it in the Aga

ovens, otherwise it will always be hot and therefore not suitable for its intended use. Remove the shelf from the oven as soon as cooking is complete and allow it to cool down – I usually put mine just outside the back door until cold, and then store it close to the Aga ready for use again.

AGA ADORATION

Your Aga is there to work, not to be polished and adored! However, a little tender loving care will keep it splatter-free and ready to perform the weekly tasks of drying and airing the washing just as readily as cooking the dinner. Do wipe the top over regularly, and if it should become necessary to do some serious cleaning, a non-abrasive cream cleaner will remove most unpleasantness.

After using the Aga toaster you may need to brush the Boiling Plate with the wire brush to remove crumbs. Whenever my kettle is slow to boil I know that there is still some breakfast on the Boiling Plate! I also use the wire brush regularly on the floor of the ovens, particularly the Roasting Oven. This is because I do a good deal of cooking, especially baking, directly on the oven floor and, if there are any boil-overs, bubble-ups or flour deposits, the oven can quickly begin to look as if it has been used for ritualistic burnings. The wire shelves revive beautifully after minimal attention with a gentle scourer and hot, soapy water.

GOOD THINGS TO GET

Top quality flat- or ground-based pans are essential for efficient use of the Aga. Agaluxe pans are ideal, especially as they have unique flat lids which enable them to be stacked in the oven to maximise the space. A ridged grill pan, beloved of TV chefs, is a good Aga accessory, both for contemporary presentation and for grilling on the floor of the Roasting Oven. Pre-cut baking liners are available for the Aga roasting tins and other standard cake tins, and keen bakers may also find the Aga Cake Baker invaluable. However, all the quick bakes included in this book can be baked with the standard Aga equipment or regular baking tins.

Cooking in the Aga often involves using pans in the ovens and it is a good idea to invest in some pan handle covers. Handles are for holding and we all make a grab for them, even when we know they are hot. It's a good idea to get into the habit of putting a handle cover on and leaving it there, especially if you are moving a pan from the oven to one of the Aga plates, before transferring it, say, to the Simmering Oven. An oven glove that you take away is not nearly as safe as a handle cover.

Aga gauntlets are long-sleeved oven gloves and a very worthwhile investment; great for ferreting around in the back of ovens to retrieve 'lost' dishes.

IMPOSSIBLY CHINTZY BUT USEFUL THINGS TO DO WITH YOUR AGA

Like so many before me I have fallen into describing the Aga as a way of life, for so it is. And if you don't end up doing at least some of the following with your Aga I shall be amazed:

☆ Red wine can be brought to room temperature by the side of the Aga – don't actually put it on the Aga as it may get too hot.

☆ Citrus fruits become far more juicy if warmed on the top of the Aga for a few minutes before squeezing.

☆ Seeds can be germinated under cling film on the work surface around your Aga – a useful extension to an unheated greenhouse.

☆ Olive oil which has clouded through cold can be gently warmed back to clarity near the Aga.

☆ Hardened, impossible-to-spread honey can be warmed gently, either on top of the Aga or in a small pan of hot water on the floor of the Simmering Oven.

☆ Damp washing can be dried ready for ironing on top of the Simmering Plate, which is also a good place for airing the laundry. I must confess to no longer ironing boxer shorts since the Aga was installed, but I cannot subscribe to those who don't iron their sheets! There are, however, lots of people who I am convinced would own an Aga solely for this benefit.

☆ Wet shoes from early morning dog walks dry quickly in front of the Aga – much better than leaving them to go into the fireplace in the evening once the fire has been lit.

☆ A basket of damp logs will dry out by the side of the Aga, ready to light the fire.

☆ Damp dogs will also dry quickly, as above. But don't expect all dogs to take instantly to lying in front of an Aga – Toby Moon never considered it until we visited some friends who had a cotton rug in front of theirs, from which he hardly moved all evening! So we now have a cotton rug in front of ours (or do I mean his?) but I do suggest that you choose a rug that can be stuffed in the washing machine whenever necessary.

Above all, however, the Aga is for cooking. I hope that you will enjoy the recipes that I have included in this book of contemporary favourites, a mixture of internationally influenced creations and nursery favourites to suit all tastes.

JUST A WORD ABOUT THE RECIPES

Some of the ingredient lists may look dauntingly long, but do remember that many of them are for complete dishes including all the vegetables. Very often a goodly number of herbs, spices and seasonings are needed to create the right balance of flavours, and

these make the recipe look very involved. I have written everything out in as straightforward a way as possible – if you have a well-stocked spice drawer and an average store cupboard, you will probably find that you need shop for little more than the fresh ingredients. In case you have trouble with any of the shopping I have included a few useful mail order addresses at the end of the book.

Bone-in beef: these recipes were tested – and drooled over – before the 1997 UK ban on bone-in beef. In the hope that this law will be short-lived I have left my recipes for rib roast and oxtail and trust that you will soon be able to choose to make them yourself.

In the sections headed Aga Equipment, please note that the position of the runners is counted from the top – in other words, the first set of runners is at the top of the oven, and the third or fourth set is at the bottom.

COMPLETE MEAL PLANNING

I have deliberated long and hard about including a selection of complete menus in this book, but have come down against it because I have yet to meet anyone who has used such a guide! However, there are a few basic rules to consider when you are cooking large quanitities or a feast in your Aga:

☆ Choose a variety of dishes that do not all need last-minute, stove-top attention.

☆ Cook as much as you can in the Aga ovens – remember, more stored heat will be used or wasted if you cook on the top.

☆ Ensure that your vegetable selection includes some root vegetables which can be cooked in the Simmering Oven.

☆ Pre-heat a wok on the floor of the Roasting Oven before stir-frying on the Boiling Plate.

☆ Agaluxe, flat-topped pans that can be stacked are the most efficient way of utilisng the space in the Aga ovens.

☆ Most casseroles benefit from being reheated the day after cooking – this allows the flavours to mingle and blend to perfection. It also means that there will be more stored heat available for on-the-day cooking.

☆ Leave pans of water for vegetables, pasta etc on the back of the Aga to warm up before you need to bring them to the boil – this will cut down the cooking/heating time.

☆ Aga hotplate cookery is fine when only one or two dishes are to be cooked.

Rosemary Moon.

Soups and Starters

Roasted Pumpkin,
Cinnamon & Lovage Soup

Just two villages away from me, in Slindon, lives one of the most extraordinary horticulturists I know – Mr Upton, the Pumpkin Man. In autumn, the walls and yard of his cottage groan under the weight of a fantastic display of pumpkins, squashes and gourds of all sizes, colours and descriptions. The Aga has proved a delight for cooking his produce, and this is one of my favourite pumpkin soups – try serving it with fingers of Devilled Leek and Goats' Cheese Toasts (page 17).

1 Remove the seeds from the squash then arrange the slices, boat-like, in the roasting tin. Season well and drizzle with olive oil, then roast for about 1 hour, until the squash is tender. Cool slightly, then scoop the flesh out of the skins and chop it roughly.

2 Meanwhile, heat 2 tablespoons of olive oil and the butter in a large oven-to-hob casserole on the Simmering Plate. Add the onion and cook until soft but not browned, then add the cinnamon and cook for a further 1 minute. Stir the squash into the pan with the stock, lovage and a little more salt and pepper, then bring the soup to the boil. Cover and transfer to the floor of the Simmering Oven for at least 1 hour, but preferably two.

3 Cool the soup slightly, then blend it until smooth. Add any extra seasonings necessary, then serve with a swirl of cream and a little extra finely chopped lovage.

Serves 6–8

6 thick slices Crown Prince or
    other firm-fleshed squash,
    weighing 1.5kg
salt and freshly ground
    black pepper
2 tbsp fruity olive oil, plus extra
    for drizzling
1 large onion, finely sliced
25g butter
1 tsp ground cinnamon
2.3 litres/9 cups well-flavoured
    vegetable stock
2 tbsp young lovage leaves or
    flat-leafed parsley, roughly
    chopped
single cream and finely chopped
    lovage leaves, to serve

Aga equipment:

small roasting tin on third set of
    runners in Roasting Oven

Onion, Chilli & Couscous Soup

Couscous is an excellent, if unusual, way to thicken a spicy clear soup. If you're a chilli freak you can make this as hot as you like by adding extra fire pods but, be warned, it's pretty hot as it is!

Serves 4

2 tbsp olive oil
large knob of butter
4 large onions, finely sliced
½ tsp mild chilli powder
1 tsp ground ginger
½ tsp ground turmeric
2 bay leaves
1 small fresh red chilli,
seeded and finely chopped
3–4 cloves garlic,
finely sliced
1 litre/4 cups good chicken
or vegetable stock
1 tsp salt
freshly ground black pepper
50g/⅓ cup couscous

1 Heat the oil and butter together in an oven-to-hob casserole on the floor of the Roasting Oven while preparing the onions. Add the onions, stirring them into the hot fat, then cook, uncovered, for about 45 minutes on the oven floor, stirring once or twice. *To get the right flavour and richness in this soup it is essential to cook the onions until they are really well browned, so persevere for as long as necessary.* Add the spices, bay leaves, chilli and garlic, and then cook for a further 5 minutes.

2 Pour the stock into the pan, then bring the soup quickly to the boil on top of the Aga. Cover and cook on the floor of the Simmering Oven for at least 1 hour, but preferably two.

3 Stir the couscous into the soup, then return it to the Simmering Oven for a further 30 minutes. Remove the bay leaves, then season to taste and serve.

Butter Bean & Butternut Soup

I first tasted butternut squash when staying with my friend Linda in South Africa. She made it into soup flavoured with orange, but I have combined it with creamy butter beans for a very substantial main course soup.

1 Cut the squash in half lengthways, scoop out the seeds and place the squash in the small roasting tin. Season lightly and drizzle with olive oil, then roast for 40 minutes.

2 Rinse the butter beans then bring them to the boil in a pan of fresh water – use just enough to cover the beans. Cover and place on the floor of the Simmering Oven until required.

3 Pour any oil and juices from the squash into a large oven-to-hob casserole and add sufficient olive oil to give about 2 tablespoons. Cook the onion in the oil, covered, for 10 minutes on the floor of the Roasting Oven, then add the garlic. Scoop the flesh out of the squash and add it to the pan with the butter beans and their water. Add the stock cube or bouillon powder, grated nutmeg and a little extra salt and pepper, with sufficient extra water to cover the ingredients. Return the soup to the boil, then cover and cook on the floor of the Simmering Oven for at least 1 hour, until the butter beans are tender.

4 Allow the soup to cool slightly, then whizz it until smooth in a blender or food processor, adding the milk. Return to the pan and reheat as necessary, adding extra salt, pepper and nutmeg to taste.

Serves 6–8

1 medium butternut squash
salt and freshly ground
    black pepper
olive oil
175g/1 cup butter beans
    or lima beans, soaked
    overnight
1 large onion, finely chopped
1 clove garlic, crushed
1 vegetable stock cube
    or 1 tsp vegetable
    bouillon powder
½ freshly grated nutmeg
500ml/2½ cups milk

Aga equipment:

small roasting tin on
    second set of runners in
    Roasting Oven

Devilled Leek & Goats' Cheese Toasts

Piquant and delicious, these unusual toasts stand alone as a nibble, could be served with a salad garnish as a starter, or may be cut into fingers and served as very special croutons with a soup.

Serves 4–6

3 large leeks, weighing about 450g, trimmed and washed
3 tbsp fruity olive oil
1–2 cloves garlic, finely sliced
1 tsp cayenne pepper
1 tbsp wholegrain mustard
75g mild soft goats' cheese
salt and freshly ground black pepper
3–4 cold crisp slices of wholewheat toast

Aga equipment:

wire shelf on second set of runners in Roasting Oven

1 Hold the leeks upside down under running water to wash them – this stops the grit going back into the leeks.

2 Heat the oil in a large frying pan on the floor of the Roasting Oven while slicing the leeks very finely. Add the leeks to the oil with the garlic and cayenne and cook, covered, on the oven floor for 12–15 minutes, until well softened, stirring once or twice.

3 Add the mustard and cheese to the leeks and stir until melted together, then season to taste.

4 Just before serving, pile the leek mixture on to the toasts and cook on a baking sheet at the top of the Roasting Oven for 8–10 minutes, until lightly browned and set. Cut the crusts off the toasts or leave them on, according to your own preference.

Roasted Pepper Salad

When I was a child I don't think my mother ever bought a pepper, but now they are almost a staple part of the British diet! Roasting and removing the pepper skins neutralises any tendency to windiness, and the Aga Roasting Oven is perfect for that job.

1 Place the peppers in the roasting tin and roast for 20–30 minutes according to their size, turning once. Once the peppers are blackened all over, cover them with a clean, damp tea towel then leave them for 10–15 minutes to cool – *this helps to steam the skins free of the flesh. (I have never liked the concept of placing hot peppers in plastic bags to ease off the skins – the damp tea towel method is much better.)* Peel the peppers – start at the flower end and just pull the papery skin off, then pull out the core and seeds.

2 Rinse the peppers, cut them into strips and place in a small serving dish. Add the garlic, seasoning, oil and vinegar. Stir well, then leave to marinade for at least 1 hour. Add any extra seasoning necessary, and stir in the basil just before serving. Serve at room temperature – if the peppers are too cold you will severely retard their sweet flavour.

Serves 6

4–6 peppers of mixed
   colours
1–2 plump cloves garlic,
   finely sliced
salt and freshly ground
   black pepper
3 tbsp fruity olive oil
1 tbsp sherry vinegar
1 tbsp freshly torn basil
   leaves

Aga equipment:

small roasting tin on
   second set of runners in
   Roasting Oven

Nachos

An informal Tex-Mex starter to keep going back to over a drink with friends.

1 Blend together the cheese and soured cream. Arrange the chips on a suitable ovenproof serving plate or baking sheet, layered with the cheese and cream. Bake in the Roasting Oven for 5 minutes, until the cheese has melted and the chips are hot. Seed and chop the tomatoes.

2 If you have heated the chips on a baking sheet, scrape them on to a warmed serving plate.

3 Scatter with the seeded and chopped tomatoes, jalapeños and a few blobs of soured cream, if you like, then start nibbling.

Serves 4

75–100g strong Cheddar
   cheese, grated
150ml/⅔cup soured cream
200g packet nachip wafers
   or mild tortilla chips
2 tomatoes
4–5 tsp sliced pickled jalapeño
   peppers
soured cream garnish (optional)

Aga equipment:

wire shelf on third set of
   runners in Roasting Oven

Moorish Humus

*Moorish in deliciousness, but also through the Spanish influence
of oranges and fragrant olive oil.*

Serves 4–6

150g/1 cup chickpeas,
soaked overnight
4 tbsp/½ cup tahini
4 fl oz/½ cup light, floral
Spanish olive oil
2 cloves garlic, crushed
1 tsp salt
freshly ground black pepper
2 oranges, zest and
chopped flesh
1 tbsp fresh sage leaves,
roughly chopped
Spanish paprika, to garnish

1 Drain the chickpeas and rinse them thoroughly, then place in a pan and cover with fresh water. Cover and bring quickly to the boil, then cook on the Simmering Plate for 10 minutes. Drain off some of the water, leaving just enough to cover the chick peas, cover the pan and cook again on the floor of the Simmering Oven for 3½–4 hours, until the chick peas are tender. Allow them to cool, then drain off the liquid completely.

2 Purée the chick peas in a liquidiser or food processor with the remaining ingredients, adding orange juice as necessary to give a smooth but grainy thick paste. Season well, then chill only lightly for about 30 minutes before serving, drizzled with a little extra oil and sprinkled with paprika.

Artichoke, Lemon Grass & Grapefruit Soup

A soup with a most unusual flavour – hot, sour, tangy, tongue tingling.
A favourite.

Serves 4–6

1 Melt the butter into the oil in a large oven-to-hob casserole on the floor of the Roasting Oven, then add the onion and lemon grass and cook, covered, for 10 minutes.

2 Stir in the artichokes with the grapefruit zest and segments, and chilli, then add the stock. Bring the soup to the boil on top of the Aga. Season lightly, then add the lime leaves, if using. Cover and cook on the floor of the Simmering Oven for 2 hours.

3 Remove the lime leaves, if used, then whizz the soup to a smooth purée, adding sufficient milk to give the consistency that you like best. Season to taste with extra salt and pepper and reheat, if necessary, before serving.

25g butter
1 tbsp fragrant olive oil
1 large onion, finely chopped
1 stalk lemon grass, bruised
  and finely chopped
500g Jerusalem artichokes,
  washed and roughly chopped
1 large grapefruit, grated zest
  and segments
1 fresh green chilli, seeded and
  finely chopped
750ml/3 cups well-flavoured
  vegetable stock
salt and white pepper
3–4 kaffir lime leaves, fresh or
  dried (optional)
milk

Mediterranean Tomato Tarts

The best tomato dishes are made with fruits picked ripe from outdoor plants so, to get the best possible Mediterranean flavour, use the ripest ingredients for these excellent tarts. Testers' comments – Wow!

Serves 4

Pastry:

200g/1⅓ cups plain flour
pinch of salt
2 tsp rosemary, freshly chopped
4 tbsp fruity olive oil
3–4 large halves sun-dried tomatoes in oil, drained and finely shredded
cold water
salad leaves, to garnish

Filling:

1 small aubergine, cut into 8 thin slices
4–5 tbsp olive oil
1 onion or 1 small leek, finely sliced
1 clove garlic, crushed
4–6 black olives, pitted and sliced
3–4 halves sun-dried tomatoes, shredded
salt and freshly ground black pepper
4 ripe tomatoes, cored and sliced

1 Mix together the flour, salt and rosemary, then pour the olive oil into the centre and add the shredded tomatoes. Begin bringing the mixture together into a firm, manageable dough, adding a little water as necessary.

2 Divide the pastry into four and roll out to line individual 10cm tart tins. Chill the cases in the refrigerator whilst preparing the filling.

3 Heat a large frying pan on the Boiling Plate, add 3 tablespoons of the oil, then fry the aubergine slices quickly on both sides, until they are just starting to brown. Place one slice over the base of each pastry case, and reserve the others.

4 Transfer the frying pan pan to the Simmering Plate, add another spoonful of oil, the leek and garlic, and cook slowly until softened. Remove from the heat and stir in the olives, sun-dried tomatoes and seasonings. Divide the mixture between the tarts and top with the remaining aubergine slices.

5 Slice the tomatoes and arrange them over the filling, finishing with a little salt, pepper and a pinch of sugar if the tomatoes have not ripened naturally on the vine. Drizzle a little extra olive oil over the tomatoes if your conscience will allow, then bake for 15–20 minutes on the floor of the Roasting Oven. Serve warm with a small salad garnish.

Carrot, Lentil & Orange Soup
WITH ORANGE SALSA

A vibrant orange soup with a very bright flavour. Served with a hearty hunk of fresh bread, this soup makes a meal in itself.

1 Cook the onions in the oil in a large covered pan on the floor of the Roasting Oven. Add the carrots and cook, covered, for a further 5 minutes.

2 Stir the lentils into the pan with some seasoning and the stock. Bring quickly to the boil on top of the Aga, then cover and cook for 2½–3 hours on the floor of the Simmering Oven.

3 Prepare the salsa while the soup is cooking. Heat a frying pan on the Boiling Plate until evenly hot, then dry fry the mustard seeds until starting to pop. Allow to cool slightly, then mix them with the remaining salsa ingredients and a little salt and pepper. Leave the salsa to stand for at least 1 hour before serving. This allows the flavours to blend.

4 Liquidise the soup with the orange zest, then reheat it before serving, if necessary. Stir in the orange juice and coriander at the last moment, then serve the soup with a good spoonful of salsa in each serving.

Serves 6

2 onions, chopped
3 tbsp olive oil
500g carrots, roughly
   chopped
125g/¾ cup orange lentils
salt and freshly ground
   black pepper
1.2 litres/5 cups well-
   flavoured vegetable stock
1 orange, grated zest
   and juice
1 tbsp coriander,
   freshly chopped

Salsa:

1 tbsp white mustard seeds
1 orange, grated zest and
   chopped flesh
2 tomatoes, seeded
   and chopped
1 clove garlic, finely chopped
4 spring onions, trimmed and
   chopped
1 small green pepper,
   seeded and finely chopped
1 tbsp coriander, freshly
   chopped

Pancetta Roast Quail

WITH FIELD MUSHROOMS ON TOAST

Oven-ready quail are available in most large supermarkets if you don't have your own source of birds from a shoot. They are so simple to cook, but make a suitably impressive and sophisticated starter for the smartest of parties – so long as your guests are happy to use their fingers. Remember to put out the finger bowls!

Serves 4

4 oven-ready quail
4 rashers pancetta or streaky bacon
salt and freshly ground black pepper
melted butter
4 large field mushrooms, peeled and stalks removed
4 slices freshly cooked hot buttered toast, crusts removed
salad leaves, to serve
freshly chopped parsley, to garnish

Mustard vinaigrette:

4 tbsp olive oil
1 tbsp sherry vinegar
1 tsp sweet or Dijon mustard
1 tsp sugar, or to taste
salt and freshly ground black pepper

Aga equipment:

wire shelf on third set of runners in Roasting Oven

1 Wrap each quail in a rasher of pancetta then place them in a shallow tin. Brush with melted butter and season lightly, then roast for 25 minutes. While the quail are cooking, whisk all the ingredients for the vinaigrette together.

2 Brush the mushrooms with a little butter and add them to the tin with the quail for the last 10 minutes of cooking time.

3 To serve, toss the salad leaves in a little of the dressing and arrange them on slightly warmed plates. Snip away the string from the quail, trying to leave the pancetta in tact. Place a mushroom on each slice of toast and place on the salad. Place a quail on top, then spoon a little more mustard dressing over and garnish with chopped parsley. Serve immediately.

Quesadillas

A kind of Mexican pizza which can be as spicy as you wish. I like to use a blue Brie but you can choose your favourite cheese, and add as much chilli as you like. Try replacing the avocado with sliced mango, drizzled with fresh lime juice.

1 Thinly slice the Brie and remove the rinds if preferred. Finely chop the avocado. Seed and chop the tomatoes. Seed and finely chop the chilli. Trim and slice the spring onions.

2 Arrange the sliced cheese over the tortillas on baking sheets, then cook for 5 minutes.

3 Scatter the avocado, tomato, chilli and onion over, then cut the tortillas into four pizza-like wedges to serve.

Serves 4

200g blue Brie
1 small avocado
2 tomatoes
1 fresh red chilli
2–3 spring onions
4 flour tortillas

Aga equipment:

wire shelf on third set of
    runners in Roasting Oven

Mixed Mushrooms
IN A SESAME BOX

Inspired by Chef-Patron Nik Westacott at Platters Restaurant in Chichester, this is a recipe devised by a fungi fanatic to celebrate the wild mushroom season. It can also be made with regular cultivated mushrooms, or a selection of the exotic fungi available in supermarkets. You could always soak a few dried porcini and add them to button mushrooms.

1 Roll out the pastry until 6mm thick, then cut it into four oblongs about 7.5x12.5cm. Place the pastry on a large baking sheet and carefully mark a rim of about 1cm around each box. Brush with egg and scatter with sesame seeds. Don't let the egg seal the edges of the pastry, otherwise it will not puff up in the Aga.

2 Bake for 12 minutes, or until the boxes are a light golden brown. Carefully cut away the centres of the boxes to form lids.

Serves 6

250g packet of puff pastry
1 egg, beaten
sesame seeds
chives and salad leaves, to
    garnish

Filling:

4 spring onions, trimmed
    and sliced

2 tbsp olive oil
500g mixed fresh mushrooms
½ tsp ground mace
salt and freshly ground
black pepper
4 tbsp crème fraîche or
double cream

Aga equipment:

wire shelf on third set of
runners in Roasting Oven

2 Prepare the mushroom filling while the pastry is baking. Cook the onions in the oil in a frying pan on the Simmering Plate until they are soft, then add the sliced mushrooms and stir-fry for 3–4 minutes. Add the mace, a little seasoning and the cream, then continue heating until piping hot.

3 Spoon the mushrooms into the prepared boxes and replace the lids. Serve with a salad leaf garnish, with the chives sticking up out of the boxes.

Quick Roasted Tomato Bruschettas

A romantically Mediterranean version of an old favourite – grilled tomatoes on toast! For a slightly more substantial feast, top the tomatoes with thin slices of mozzarella just before baking, then drizzle the cheese with olive oil before serving. Chopped olives, capers or mushrooms can be added to the basic marinated tomatoes for a more original bruschetta.

Serves 4
1 large clove garlic
8 slices ciabatta
6–8 of the ripest, reddest
tomatoes, seeded
and chopped
1 tbsp finely chopped shallot
or onion
3 tbsp fruity olive oil
salt and freshly ground
black pepper
6 fresh basil leaves, torn

Aga equipment:

wire shelf on second set of
runners in Simmering Oven,
then wire shelf on second set
of runners in Roasting Oven

1 Cut the garlic and rub the cut surface over the ciabatta slices. Place the bread on a baking sheet and dry in the Simmering Oven for 30 minutes.

2 Crush the same garlic over the tomatoes, then add the onion and olive oil with a little salt and pepper and leave to marinade while the ciabatta is in the Simmering Oven. Stir in the basil, then pile the tomatoes on to the ciabatta slices.

3 Bake the bruschettas quickly in the Roasting Oven for 10 minutes, then serve immediately.

Fish and Shellfish

Fresh Tuna & Spinach Risotto

Most people overcook fresh tuna making it tough and tasteless. It should be moist and full of flavour, which is achieved by a light cooking after marinating in a pungent brew.

1 Mix together all the ingredients for the marinade, then add the tuna and turn the steaks in the mixture. Leave for at least 1 hour. Remove the tuna steaks. Mix the olive oil with the remaining marinade, then add the onion and cook in a large covered frying pan on the floor of the Roasting Oven for 5 minutes.

2 Stir the rice into the pan until the grains are well coated with the hot oil, then add the hot stock. Cook, covered, on the floor of the Roasting Oven for 20–25 minutes, adding the shredded spinach after 15 minutes and giving the rice a stir. The rice will absorb the stock, leaving a creamy, moist risotto.

3 Preheat a ridged grill pan just before adding the spinach to the rice. Brush the pan with a little oil, then preheat it on the Boiling Plate until very hot – this will take about 5 minutes. Brown the tuna quickly on both sides. Transfer the tuna in the pan to the shelf in the Roasting Oven and cook for a further 4–5 minutes. Flake the fish with a fork, then add it to the risotto with seasonings to taste.

4 Top the risotto with shavings of fresh Parmesan cheese and serve immediately.

Serves 4

2 fresh tuna steaks, about
   175g each, skin removed
2 tbsp olive oil
1 red onion, finely sliced
250g/1½ cups risotto rice
1.2 litres/5 cups hot
   vegetable or fish stock
125g fresh spinach, finely
   shredded
salt and freshly ground
   black pepper
Parmesan shavings, to serve

Marinade:

3 tbsp fruity olive oil
1 lime, grated zest and juice
4 spring onions, trimmed and
   finely sliced
salt and freshly ground
   black pepper

RISOTTO RICE

The most common risotto rices are Arborio, Vialone Nano or Carnaroli, all of which are far more expensive than regular rice but worth every penny as they produce such wonderful finished dishes. If your rice is purchased in a cloth bag, try to store it in that – rice does not really need to be kept in an air-tight container, unless it's to keep small, furry visitors out!

Almond-Coated Fish Cakes

I think these are the best fish cakes I have ever made – they are light and the finely diced fish lends an interesting texture instead of the usual mash. I strongly recommend using some New Zealand hoki which is available from most fish counters – it has a good firm flesh which contrasts well with other more local white fish.

Serves 4

125g/2 cups fresh wholewheat or white breadcrumbs
milk
1 small leek, very finely sliced
3–4 tbsp mildly flavoured olive oil
500g mixed white fish fillets such as hoki, haddock, plaice or sole, skinned
1 large egg, beaten
1–2 tbsp tarragon, freshly chopped
1 tbsp parsley, freshly chopped
salt and white pepper
2–3 tbsp mayonnaise
salad leaves, to serve

Coating:

50g/⅔ cup fresh wholewheat or white breadcrumbs
50g ground almonds

1 Soak the breadcrumbs for the fish cakes in milk for a few minutes to soften them, then squeeze them dry and discard the milk. Cook the leek in 1 tablespoon of the oil in a large frying pan for 4–5 minutes on the floor of the Roasting Oven until just soft but not browned.

2 Cut the fish into 6mm dice – *this is important as the fish is not pre-cooked in this recipe.* Mix with the breadcrumbs, leek and all the other ingredients, adding just enough mayonnaise to give a soft but manageable mixture.

3 Mix the almonds and breadcrumbs for the coating together. Divide the fish mixture into twelve and shape firmly into cakes, coating them in the almond crumbs. Press the crumbs firmly into the surface of the cakes and don't use flour on your hands unless absolutely necessary.

4 Heat the remaining oil in the leek pan on the floor of the Roasting Oven, then add the fish cakes and cook them for 4–5 minutes on each side, again on the floor of the oven. *The fish cakes will doubtless need to be cooked in two batches, so keep the first lot warm in the Simmering Oven while cooking the others.* Serve immediately with a small tossed salad.

Tuna Tart
WITH SPICED YOGHURT DRESSING
& WARM CELERY SALAD

This is informal, inexpensive summer eating at its best – a warm tuna and egg mélange in short, crumbly pastry, served with a tangy dressing and the simplest of warm celery salads.

1 Prepare the pastry. Rub the butter into the flour and salt, then add the beaten egg and sufficient cold water to bind the pastry into a stiff dough. Knead lightly on a floured surface, then roll out about two-thirds of the pastry into a circle and use it to line the base and sides of a deep, 20cm loose-bottomed sandwich tin. Chill the pastry while preparing the filling.

2 Cook the onion in the butter and oil in a small pan on the floor of the Roasting Oven, for just 4–5 minutes, until soft. Add all the remaining ingredients for the filling, moistening the mixture with 2–3 tbsp olive oil, if necessary. *The mixture should be mouth-wateringly moist, but not soggily wet.*

3 Spoon the filling into the chilled pastry case, then roll out the remaining dough to cover the tart. Damp the edges of the pastry with water, then knock them together and pinch the crust to give an attractive edge to the tart. Make a hole in the centre of the pastry with a sharp knife, to let the steam escape from the filling and keep the pastry crisp. Make any trimmings into leaves or fishes to decorate the tart, if you feel so inclined.

4 Bake the tart on the floor of the Roasting Oven for 40 minutes, sliding the cold shelf on to the third set of runners after 25 minutes. Give the tart a half turn at the same time. If you are using a four-oven Aga, bake the tart for 15 mintues in the Roasting Oven, then for a further 30–40 minutes on the floor of the Baking Oven.

5 Make the celery salad as soon as the tart has gone into the Aga. Place all the ingredients in a small pan with just enough water to cover, then bring quickly to the boil. Cover the pan and leave it on the back of the Aga until required.

Serves 6

Pastry:

150g butter, chopped small
300g/2⅓ cups plain flour
1 tsp salt
1 large egg, beaten

Filling:

1 small onion, finely chopped
15g butter
1 tbsp oil
4 hard-boiled eggs, finely chopped
200g can tuna, drained and flaked
1 lemon, grated zest and juice
1 tbsp capers, roughly chopped
2–3 tbsp parsley, freshly chopped
salt and freshly ground black pepper

Salad:

4–6 sticks celery, depending on size
1–2 cloves garlic, peeled but left whole
6 black peppercorns

Sauce:

2 tsp cumin seeds
200ml/1 cup natural yogurt
3 tbsp crème fraîche
1 lemon, grated zest and juice
2 tbsp coriander, freshly chopped

Aga equipment:

cold shelf on third set of
runners in Roasting Oven,
mid-way through cooking

6 Heat a frying pan on the Boiling Plate until evenly hot, then add the cumin seeds and dry roast them for just 30 seconds, until they start to pop. Turn into a mortar and or use the end of a rolling pin to crush them lightly on a chopping board. Blend the yogurt and crème fraîche together, then add the cumin and remaining sauce ingredients, with seasoning to taste.

7 Allow the tart to cool for about 10 minutes before cutting, then serve in generous wedges, topped with a dollop of the sauce and with a large spoonful of the warmed, drained salad.

Spanish-Style Squid
WITH CITRUS JUICES

I love squid, but I do despair when it is offered fried, tough and in a tasteless batter. The citrus juices give this recipe a sharp, refreshing flavour, while the pine nuts provide a crunchy textural contrast to the squid.

Serves 4

1 onion, finely chopped
25g butter
2 tbsp olive oil
2 cloves garlic, crushed
400g prepared squid rings
50g/½ cup pine nuts
250ml/1 cup dry white wine
1 lemon, grated zest
and juice
1 lime, grated zest and juice
salt and freshly ground
black pepper
flat-leaf parsley, freshly
chopped, to garnish
fresh crusty bread, to serve

1 Cook the onion in the butter and oil in a covered oven-to-hob casserole on the floor of the Roasting Oven for 10 minutes. Lift the casserole on to the Boiling Plate, then add the garlic and squid, and cook quickly until the squid is an opaque white, and the onions are just starting to brown.

2 Move the pan across to the Simmering Plate, then add the pine nuts and about half the wine. Cook until the wine has reduced by about half, then add the remaining wine and the fruit juices with a little seasoning.

3 Cover the pan and cook for 1 hour on the floor of the Simmering Oven, until the squid is meltingly tender. Season lightly to taste adding a pinch of sugar if necessary, then stir in some parsley and scatter the lemon and lime zest over as a garnish before serving with fresh crusty bread.

Crispy Spiced Brill
WITH SHREDDED GINGER SALAD

I love brill but it is not always easy to find on the slab, so you might like to try this oriental-style recipe with skate, plaice or lemon sole.

1 Pour the oil into a very large, deep pan (a Dutch oven is ideal) and heat it for 20 minutes, uncovered, on the floor of the Roasting Oven. This gets the oil almost up to temperature for deep-frying without wasting stored heat.

2 Fillet and skin the fish, then cut it into 2.5cm pieces. Mix together all the ingredients for the spiced flour, and in a separate bowl mix the lightly whisked egg white and cream.

3 Shred the carrots and turnips or mooli using the finest shredding plate on a food processor. *If you are doing this in advance, plunge the shreds and the sliced cucumber and celery into a bowl of iced water to keep them crisp.* Drain the vegetables just before frying the fish.

4 Whisk together all the ingredients for the vinaigrette, and season to taste. Cover a plate with lots of crumpled kitchen paper, ready for draining the fried fish.

5 Move the pan of hot oil up on to the Boiling Plate and continue heating until the oil has reached 180°C – the oil will quickly come up to temperature.

6 Rub the egg white and cream mixture well into the fish, then toss the fish in the spiced flour until evenly coated. Carefully drop pieces of the brill into the hot oil and fry for 2–3 minutes, until golden brown.

7 Drain the fish on the kitchen paper. Pile up the shredded vegetables in the centre of the warmed serving plates, then arrange the pieces of fried fish around, teasing the shredded vegetables up in the centre of the plate. Spoon the vinaigrette over and then serve immediately.

Serves 3–4

3 litres/13 cups sunflower oil for deep-fat frying
1kg fresh brill on the bone, or 500g brill fillets
1 large egg white, lightly beaten
1 tbsp double cream
2 carrots, peeled
1 mooli (daikon) or two small white turnips, peeled
½ cucumber, peeled, seeded and very finely sliced
2 sticks celery, very finely sliced

Spiced flour:

150g/1 cup plain flour
1 tsp salt
1 tbsp black poppy seeds
½ tsp mild chilli powder
1 tsp ground ginger

Vinaigrette:

3 tbsp sunflower oil
2 tbsp sesame oil
4cm piece fresh ginger root, grated and squeezed
2 tbsp light soy sauce
1 tsp poppy seeds
1 clove garlic, crushed

Thai Spiced Scallops
WITH GRAPEFRUIT SALSA

Some friends who definitely didn't like scallops became addicted after being the guinea pigs for this recipe! If you must use frozen scallops, defrosting them in water will help to retain some shape and texture, but fresh, unglazed scallops are definitely best. This is a quick stir-fry dish using the Boiling Plate.

Serves 6 as a starter, 3–4 as a main course

500g fresh scallops
2 tbsp groundnut oil
fresh coriander leaves

Salsa:

1 pink grapefruit
2 cloves garlic, finely chopped
1 fresh green chilli, finely chopped
2 tomatoes, seeded and chopped
1 small red onion, finely chopped
2 avocados, peeled and chopped
salt and freshly ground black pepper
2 tbsp coriander, freshly chopped
1 lime, grated zest and juice

Marinade:

1 stalk lemon grass, bruised and finely chopped
1 clove garlic, crushed
5cm piece fresh ginger root
salt and freshly ground black pepper
1 green chilli, finely chopped

1 Prepare the salsa. Zest the grapefruit, placing the shreds in a bowl, then cut the fruit in half. Juice half the fruit and set it to one side, then peel and chop the remaining flesh and add it to the zest in the bowl. Stir all the remaining salsa ingredients into the bowl, seasoning to taste, then leave to stand for at least 1 hour, to allow the flavours to mingle.

2 Add all the marinade ingredients to the reserved grapefruit juice and place in a shallow dish. Prepare the scallops by separating the roes, then removing any membrane or sand from the meat. Slice the white meat horizontally into two medallions, then marinade the scallops and roes for 30 minutes before cooking.

3 Heat a wok or large frying pan on the Boiling Plate until evenly hot – *if the Aga is busy, heat the pan on the floor of the Roasting Oven for 10 minutes, to conserve heat, then transfer it to the top of the Aga for cooking.* Add the oil, then scoop the scallops out of the marinade with a perforated spoon, straight into the wok. Stir-fry for 2–3 minutes, until just cooked, then strain the marinade into the pan and bring it quickly to the boil.

4 Serve the scallops on warm plates, with the salsa to one side and the hot marinade spooned over. Garnish with coriander leaves and serve immediately.

Mediterranean Roast Monkfish

WITH ROASTED TOMATO COULIS

Monkfish is a very meaty fish – well, that sounds like Double Dutch, but what I am trying to convey is that it has a firm texture and is very filling! I usually roast it on the bone, then carefully fillet it after cooking, before serving it sliced. The tomato coulis is utterly delicious and can be used with countless dishes. It freezes well and makes a perfect sauce base, so it is an excellent way of using up a glut of garden tomatoes.

1 To make the coulis, place the tomatoes in a single layer in the roasting tin. Scatter the onion over, then bury the garlic and herbs in the tin. Season the tomatoes well and scatter the sugar over them, then drizzle with olive oil. Roast the tomatoes for 45 minutes.

2 Meanwhile, pull any skin and membrane off the monkfish, then make 3–4 small cuts down each side of the bone on both sides of the fish with a sharp knife. Insert slivers of garlic, sprigs of rosemary and shreds of anchovy in each one, then season the fish with pepper and rub it with olive oil.

3 Brown the monkfish in 3 tablespoons of olive oil in a pan on the Boiling Plate, then transfer it to the high rack. Place the rack over the tomatoes after they have cooked for 45 minutes, pour any oil from the frying pan over and cook for a further 12–15 minutes.

4 Place the monkfish in the Simmering Oven to keep warm while finishing the coulis. Remove the rosemary sprigs, then turn the tomatoes *et al* into a food processor and blend to a smooth purée. Rub the mixture through a sieve into a clean pan, using the back of a ladle. Season to taste, then keep warm until required.

5 Cut the monkfish fillets from the bone, then slice them into medallions. Serve the monkfish on a bed of the coulis, or with it spooned over the fish.

Serves 4

2 monkfish tails, on the bone, weighing 800g–1kg
1 clove garlic
rosemary sprigs
3–4 anchovy fillets
freshly ground black pepper
olive oil

Coulis:

6–8 ripe tomatoes, halved
1 onion, roughly chopped
1–2 cloves garlic, unpeeled
8–10 basil leaves
3–4 sprigs rosemary
salt and freshly ground black pepper
1–2 tsp demerara sugar, depending on the ripeness of the tomatoes
olive oil

Aga equipment:

small roasting tin with high rack on third set of runners in Roasting Oven

Goujons of Mixed Fish WITH CHIPS!

Posh fish and chips, this version of the UK's favourite dish was inspired by a lunch at The Criterion, in Piccadilly Circus, in the days of the much-missed Bob Payton. It's fish and chips with a difference!

Serves 4

3 litres/13 cups sunflower oil for deep-frying
500g frozen oven chips
1 large egg white
1 tbsp double cream
125g/¾ cup plain flour
50g/⅓ cup sesame seeds
1 tsp ground cumin
1 tsp ground ginger
1 kilo mixed prepared fish such as salmon, plaice, squid, cut into bite-sized pieces
fresh lemon wedges and tartare sauce, to serve

Aga equipment:

wire shelf on second set of runners in Roasting Oven

1 Pour the oil into a large pan suitable for deep-frying and place it, uncovered, on the floor of the Roasting Oven to heat for 20–25 minutes. Place the frozen oven chips in a single layer on a baking sheet and bake them on the wire shelf over the pan of oil for 20 minutes, turning once.

2 Lightly whisk the egg white and add the cream, mixing well. Mix together the flour, sesame seeds, cumin and ginger. Cover a plate with plenty of crumpled kitchen paper to drain the fish.

3 Transfer the oil to the Boiling Plate and continue heating until it reaches 180°C. Rub the fish with the cream mixture, then toss the pieces in the seasoned flour. *You will need to cook the fish in two batches.* Drop the pieces carefully into the hot oil and fry for 3–4 minutes, until golden brown. Scoop the fish out with a perforated spoon and drain, then fry the second batch. Keep the cooked fish hot in the Simmering Oven.

4 Reheat the chips by dropping them into the hot oil, which will also crisp them up. Drain the chips. Pile the fish over the chips on warmed serving plates, and serve with wedges of lemon and tartare sauce.

Beach Fish Tacos

I cook a lot of Tex-Mex-style food, and I confidently predict that soft tacos are going to be The *popular Mexican dish. They are often served from stalls on Australian and Californian beaches – let's hope that happens in the UK soon!*

1 Pour the oil into a suitable pan for deep-fat frying, then heat it, uncovered, on the floor of the Roasting Oven for 20–25 minutes.

2 Heat a frying pan on the Boiling Plate until evenly hot, then toss in the cumin seeds and dry fry for just a few seconds until starting to brown and spit. Cool slightly, then crush with a pestle and mortar or with the end of a rolling pin.

3 To make the salsa, mix the cumin seeds with the remaining ingredients, then leave to stand for at least 30 minutes for the flavours to blend and develop.

4 Prepare the batter by combining the flour, oil and beer into a smooth paste with a little seasoning. Whisk the egg white until stiff and fold it into the batter just before using. Crumple lots of kitchen paper on to a plate to drain the fish after frying.

Serves 4

3 litres/13 cups sunflower oil for deep-fat frying
500g white fish fillets such as sole, plaice, whiting or brill, skinned and cut into small, bite-sized pieces
2–3 tbsp flour for dipping
8 flour tortillas, wrapped together loosely in foil
soured cream, to serve

Salsa:

1 tbsp cumin seeds
3 tomatoes, seeded and chopped
10cm chunk of cucumber, diced
1 small red onion, finely chopped
2 cloves garlic, finely chopped
1 fresh green chilli, seeded and finely chopped
2 tbsp red wine vinegar
salt and freshly ground black pepper
2–3 tbsp coriander leaves, freshly chopped

Batter:

125g/1 cup plain flour
3 tbsp sunflower oil
250ml/1 cup bitter beer
salt and freshly ground black pepper
1 egg white, whisked until stiff

Aga equipment:

wire shelf on second set of runners in Roasting Oven

5 Transfer the oil to the Boiling Plate and continue heating until it reaches 180°C. Place the foil packet of tortillas in the Roasting Oven to heat through.

6 Toss the fish in the flour then dunk the pieces into the batter. Cook the fish in the hot oil for 3–4 minutes, until the batter is crisp and golden. Drain on the crumpled kitchen paper.

7 To serve, spoon some of the salsa on to each warmed tortilla, then add pieces of fish in batter and top with sour cream. Don't be too generous or you won't be able to wrap the filling up in the tortillas. Eat instantly!

Hot Smoked Haddock & Turnip Cream

Inspired by brandade, *the rustic French dish made with salt cod, this combines the classic English ingredients of smoked haddock and turnips, which are much easier to come by than the preserved cod.*

Serves 4 as a starter

1 onion, finely chopped
450g turnips, peeled and roughly chopped
large knob of butter
1 tbsp olive oil
250ml/1 cup milk
350g smoked haddock
2–3 tbsp double or whipping cream
2 tbsp parsley, freshly chopped
1 tbsp capers, chopped
salt and freshly ground black pepper
crusty bread or oat cakes, to serve

Aga equipment:

wire shelf on third set of runners in Roasting Oven

1 Cook the onion and turnip in the butter and oil in a covered pan on the floor of the Roasting Oven for 10 minutes, then add the milk and cook for a further 5 minutes.

2 Meanwhile, skin the fish then add to the pan and place the covered pan on the floor of the Simmering Oven for 20 minutes, until the fish is cooked and the turnips are tender.

3 Remove the haddock from the pan, then drain off the milk. Whizz the onion and turnips until smooth, adding a little milk if necessary. Flake the haddock, then stir it back into the mixture, adding the cream, parsley and capers. Season well, then turn into a small buttered ovenproof dish.

4 Bake in the Roasting Oven for 10 minutes before serving with crusty bread or oatcakes.

Pan-Fried Scallops
WITH LIME & SUN-DRIED TOMATO CREAM SAUCE

Another delicious dish of scallops, this time flavoured raunchily with sun-dried tomatoes and lime. This is rich, so serve it with lightly steamed vegetables or a fresh, crisp salad and a timbale of boiled rice. A timbale is a small mould.

1 Cut the roes from the scallops, then remove any membrane and sand from the white meat before cutting each scallop horizontally into two medallions. Heat the oil and butter on the Simmering Plate, add the scallops and cook quickly on the Boiling Plate for 1–2 minutes, turning once and then adding the roes. Transfer to a warmed dish and place in the Simmering Oven.

2 Cook the spring onions in the pan juices for 1–2 minutes, then add the shredded tomatoes and stock. Bring quickly to the boil and cook until the stock has reduced by half. Add the cream and lime juice and heat gently on the Simmering Plate – *do not allow the sauce to boil*. Season to taste, then serve the scallops with the sauce spooned over, scattered with the lime zest as a garnish.

Serves 4

500g king scallops
2 tbsp olive oil
knob of butter
4 spring onions, finely chopped
8 sun-dried tomato halves, shredded
150ml/⅔ cup fish or vegetable stock
300ml/1¼ cups whipping cream
2 limes, grated zest and juice
salt and freshly ground black pepper

SUN-DRIED TOMATOES

These are pure Italian peasant food from Calabria, the southern-most tip of Italy's boot. They are sold dry but I prefer to purchase mine bottled in oil – pure olive oil if possible – as they are then easier to use and to combine with other ingredients. The tomatoes are usually shredded for use, and a little of their oil always adds extra flavour to dishes.

Once found only in exclusive delicatessens, sun-dried tomatoes quickly became a very popular ingredient and suddenly they were available everywhere. Once they were mass-produced, I felt that the quality, almost inevitably, suffered both in terms of flavour, shape and size of pieces. I now make a point of seeking out sun-dried tomato halves – these are more expensive but are softer and more pungent than some of the cheaper varieties. You will probably find them in the gourmet section of a large supermarket.

Halibut

WITH TAPENADE IN FILO PASTRY

Almost a Thirty-Minute Meal, and a delicious change from salmon in filo pastry. Use any firm-fleshed thick white fish of your choice – bass, cod or haddock are all possible alternatives to halibut.

Serves 4

185g can pitted sliced black olives, drained and chopped
1 clove garlic, crushed
2 tbsp capers, chopped
2 tsp wholegrain mustard
freshly ground black pepper
1 tsp fruity olive oil
8 sheets filo pastry, cut into 20cm/8 inch squares
25g butter, melted
4 halibut steaks, each weighing about 125g, or a 500g thick white fish fillet, cut into four
salad leaves, to garnish

Aga equipment:

wire shelf on third set of runners in Roasting Oven

1 Mix together the olives, garlic, capers and mustard. Season with a little black pepper, then add the oil and leave to stand for at least 30 minutes.

2 Melt the butter in a pan on the Simmering Plate or on the back of the Aga then brush the filo pastry with the melted butter. Stack the pastry into four lots of two, then divide the olive mixture between them. Nestle the fish on top then wrap the pastry over it, crimping the ends together into a cracker shape. Lift the filo parcels carefully on to a baking sheet, then brush them with the remaining butter. Cook in the Roasting Oven for 12 minutes, then serve immediately with a salad garnish.

TAPENADE

The classic tapenade is a paste of black olives, capers, garlic, mustard and olive oil, flavoured with thyme. It may be used as a dip, on bruschettas and other savouries, or as a base for toppings on pizzas. A spoonful stirred into a casserole at the end of cooking will add a dramatic pungency to the finished dish, and it also makes an excellent flavouring if stirred into cooked pasta to be served as an accompaniment to a well-flavoured stew. Black olive paste is a viable alternative, but it lacks the real raunchiness of tapenade.

Roast Cod
WITH BUTTERED GREENS

I don't know how many varieties of fish there are in the world, but you have to go a long way to better a really fresh piece of Channel-caught cod. This is a great spring dish, to make with Brussels sprout tops or spring greens.

1 Heat the oil and a knob of the butter together in a large frying pan on the Simmering Plate, then add the cod and brown it quickly on both sides on the Boiling Plate. Butter the roasting tin, transfer the cod to it and roast in the Roasting Oven for 12–15 minutes.

2 Bring a large pan of water to the boil, add the greens then return the water to the boil. Drain thoroughly, then add the greens to the buttery fish juices in the frying pan with 50g more butter, and stir fry until soft and glossy. Turn the greens into a colander and press out as much liquid as possible back into the frying pan. Transfer the greens to a serving dish and keep them warm on the back of the Aga or in the Simmering Oven.

3 Add the chopped orange flesh and the juice to the pan juices, and boil rapidly until reduced and slightly syrupy. Beat in the chilled butter, a little at a time, until the sauce is thick and glossy. Remove from the heat and add the herbs and orange zest, and season to taste.

4 Divide the cod into four thick portions, then serve on a bed of the buttered greens on warmed plates, with the sauce spooned over.

Serves 4

3 tbsp fragrant olive oil
75g butter
600g piece thick cod fillet, skinned
600g spring greens, washed, shaken dry and shredded

Orange sauce:

2 oranges, zest grated and flesh chopped
325ml/1½ cups orange juice,
25g or more of chilled butter, cut into slivers
2 tbsp freshly chopped soft herbs such as chervil, tarragon, dill
salt and freshly ground black pepper

Aga equipment:

small roasting tin on third set of runners in Roasting Oven

Turbot WITH WATERCRESS AND SPRING ONION MAYONNAISE

Turbot is one of my favourite fish, but it is very expensive, so this is a dish for special occasions only. Alternatively, you could use halibut steaks, or large plaice fillets. A small turbot is referred to as a chicken turbot – if you live near the sea, make friends with a fisherman.

Serves 4

knob of butter
2 tbsp olive oil
8 small fillets of turbot, weighing about 100g each
40g walnuts, finely chopped

Watercress mayonnaise:

75g watercress, very finely chopped
3–4 spring onions, very finely chopped
2 tbsp parsley, freshly chopped
6 tbsp mayonnaise
3 tbsp natural yogurt or crème fraîche
salt and freshly ground black pepper

Aga equipment:

wire shelf on second set of runners in Roasting Oven

1 Stir all the watercress mayonnaise ingredients together in a bowl and season to taste.

2 Heat the butter and oil together in a large frying pan on the Boiling Plate, then add the fish fillets and cook them, skin side up, for about 1 minute, until just starting to brown – the fillets will release easily when they are ready. Transfer them, skin side down, to a well-buttered baking sheet, then roast for a further 3–4 minutes in the Roasting Oven until just cooked.

3 Add the chopped walnuts to any juices left in the frying pan and heat gently on the Simmering Plate until required.

4 Scatter the walnuts over the turbot and serve with a generous amount of the watercress mayonnaise. New potatoes and a salad, or stir-fried mange touts with shreds of carrot would be ideal side servings.

Spiced Fillets of Monkfish

If you think fish is bland, try this! Serve with a robust salad which includes some mustard leaves, and perhaps a rice salad as well. Monkfish and mustard are delicious together.

1 Skin the monkfish by pulling off any papery membrane – *this is quite difficult to do, but it makes the fish much less chewy if you can get it all off.* Place the fillets on a plate, folding over any very thin pieces towards the tail to make evenly shaped fillets.

2 Mix all the spices together. Heat a heavy frying pan for a few minutes on the Boiling Plate until evenly hot, then add the spices and cook for a few seconds until fragrant and starting to pop. Crush the spices roughly with a pestle and mortar or with the end of a rolling pin.

3 Melt the butter gently, then add the mustard, seasonings and lemon juice. Brush a little of the mixture over the bottom of the roasting tin, then liberally brush the monkfish with the remainder. Press the crushed spices into the butter and place the monkfish in the roasting tin.

4 Roast the monkfish for 10 minutes in the Roasting Oven. Carve the fillets into medallions on a board. Add the cream to any spices and juices left in the bottom of the roasting tin and heat on the Simmering Plate. Serve the monkfish with the cream spooned over – *you could add an extra teaspoon of mustard to the sauce if the idea appeals.*

Serves 2

2 monkfish fillets, weighing about 500g
2 tsp crushed black peppercorns
1 tsp fennel seeds
1 tsp cumin seeds
1 tbsp coriander seeds
1 tbsp mustard seeds
50g softened butter
1 tbsp Dijon Pepper mustard or whole grain mustard
salt and freshly ground black pepper
juice of half a lemon
4 tbsp whipping cream

Aga equipment:

small roasting tin on second set of runners in Roasting Oven

Smoked Sea Bass Cutlets
WITH ANCHOVY BUTTER

I have very few gadgets in my kitchen but I was always very fond of my hot smoker, a thin-based pan which I used for smoking salmon, lamb and eggs on my previous cooker. I was delighted to work out how to achieve a lightly smoked effect in the Aga – you will need smoker chips, which you should be able to get in most good hardware stores, or use hardwood shavings if you are into DIY. The smoking is very mild – just a delicious background flavour.

Serves 4

4 large sea bass cutlets, each weighing about 175–200g
3–4 tbsp wood chips for home smokers

Anchovy butter:

125g butter
1 tbsp parsley, freshly chopped
50g can anchovy fillets, drained and finely chopped
freshly ground black pepper

Aga equipment:

small roasting tin and low wire rack

1 Prepare the anchovy butter. Cream the butter until soft, then beat in the parsley, anchovies and pepper to taste. Shape into a roll, then wrap in cling film and chill for at least 30 minutes.

2 Preheat the small roasting tin on the floor of the Roasting Oven for 20–25 minutes. Arrange the bass on the wire rack in the low position. *Remember to butter the rack first to prevent the fish from sticking to it.* Place the hot roasting tin on the Boiling Plate, then scatter the wood chips all over it – they should start to smoke almost immediately. Place the wire rack in the tin, then cover it loosely with foil – *protect your hands with your Aga gauntlets, as the tin will be very hot.*

3 Leave the tin on the Boiling Plate for 8–10 minutes, then transfer it to the floor of the Roasting Oven for a further 5–10 minutes, until the bass is just cooked through. Serve the fish with slices of anchovy butter.

43

Thirty-Minute Meals

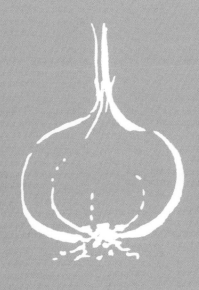

Sausages WITH RED WINE
BEAN SAUCE AND GARLIC & OLIVE
CRUSHED POTATOES

There are some wonderful sausages available now which are a feast in themselves, however you cook them. Crushed potatoes or garlic and olive oil mash are the perfect accompaniments.

1 Only prick the sausages if they are made with synthetic skins – *most designer bangers are in natural skins which will not burst during cooking.* Place them in the roasting tin and cook for 30 minutes in the Roasting Oven.

2 Just cover the potatoes with water in a saucepan and bring quickly to the boil, then cook for 5 minutes on the Simmering Plate. Drain off most of water then place the covered pan on the floor of Simmering Oven for 10–15 minutes, until the potatoes are just tender.

3 Make the sauce while the sausages and potatoes are in the Aga. Cook the onion in the olive oil in a covered frying pan on the Simmering Plate for 3–4 minutes. Add the garlic, then the wine and cook quickly on the Boiling Plate until the wine has reduced slightly, then stir in the beans and tomato purée. Season the sauce to taste, then place in the Simmering Oven until required.

4 Drain the potatoes, then heat them in the pan on the Simmering Plate for a few seconds, to drive off any surplus water and to dry them completely. Crush them lightly with a fork or a masher, then add all the remaining ingredients. Stir well and season to taste.

5 Serve the sausages with the potatoes, with the red wine and bean sauce spooned over the bangers. A small salad garnish is all that is needed to complete the meal.

Serves 4

8 large sausages of your
   favourite variety
salad leaves, to garnish

Potatoes:

500g new potatoes, scrubbed
   and roughly chopped
2–3 tbsp fruity olive oil
salt and freshly ground
   black pepper
1 large clove garlic, crushed
2 tomatoes, seeded and
   roughly chopped
25g/⅛ cup pitted black olives,
   roughly chopped

Sauce:

1 onion, finely chopped
2 tbsp olive oil
1 clove garlic, crushed
250ml/1 cup red wine
400g can flageolet beans,
   drained and rinsed
2–3 tbsp tomato purée
salt and freshly ground
   black pepper

Aga equipment:

small roasting tin on
   second set of runners in
   Roasting Oven

Gammon & Cracked Wheat Risotto

An excellent way of using up the scraps from a gammon or bacon joint, but you could just as well use cooked pork or chicken. Cracked wheat cooks up into a deliciously nutty-textured dish, and is more tolerant of not-quite-exact amounts of liquid than rice – especially useful when cooking in a hurry. I have cooked this dish completely on the top of the Aga – but it could easily be done on the floor of the Roasting Oven if you have other things cooking and wish to conserve the stored heat.

Serves 4

1 large onion, finely sliced
2 tbsp olive oil
1 medium head celery, roughly chopped – keep the leaves for garnish
2 cloves garlic, crushed
200g/1 cup cracked wheat
400g can chopped tomatoes
450ml/2 cups vegetable stock
salt and freshly ground black pepper
225g cooked diced gammon or any other cold meat

1 Cook the onion in the oil in a large frying pan on the Simmering Plate for 2–3 minutes, then add the celery, garlic and cracked wheat. Tip in the tomatoes, then add the stock with a little seasoning and bring quickly to the boil. Cook for 5 minutes on the Simmering Plate, then add the gammon and cook for a further 10–15 minutes, until the wheat has absorbed most of the stock and is a moist, risotto-like mixture in the pan.

2 Add extra seasoning if necessary, then garnish with the celery leaves and serve immediately.

CRACKED WHEAT

Often referred to as burghul or bulgur, this versatile cereal is the basis of taboulleh, a heavily minted salad garnished with spring onions, cucumber and chopped tomatoes. I like to cook with the wheat and often make it into a risotto-like dish. Its flavour and texture make it an excellent accompaniment to spicy meat dishes such as kebabs. Olive oil is needed in some quantity to moisten and flavour the grains if used as a salad.

Thai Chicken Curry

Thai curries luxuriate in the fragrance of coconut, the sourness of lemon grass and are seasoned with fish sauce – an essential Thai ingredient that is now available in most supermarkets as well as ethnic grocers. Use half a teaspoon of dried galangal root if you cannot get hold of the fresh root.

1 Heat the oil in a large frying pan on the Boiling Plate. Add the chicken and cook until lightly browned – move the pan across to the Simmering Plate if browning too quickly.

2 While the chicken is cooking make the curry paste. Seed and chop the green chillis. Roughly chop the onion and garlic. Bruise the lemon grass and roughly chop. If you have been able to get fresh galangal, peel and chop roughly. Whizz these together in a processor with the rest of the ingredients into a thick curry paste.

3 Scrape the curry paste over the chicken and bring it to the boil. Cover the pan and transfer it to the floor of the Roasting Oven for 15–20 minutes, until the chicken is cooked through and tender. Season to taste, then serve with rice or chapattis.

Serves 4

2 tbsp groundnut oil
500g boneless, skinless
    chicken breast fillets, diced
rice or chapattis, to serve

Curry paste:

2 mild fresh green chillies,
1 good handful fresh coriander
    leaves (some stalks are fine)
3cm piece fresh galangal root
1 large onion
2–3 cloves garlic
2 kaffir lime leaves
1 stalk fresh lemon grass
2 tbsp coconut milk powder
250ml/1 cup warm water
1 tbsp fish sauce
1 tsp demerara sugar
salt to taste

Fresh Pasta
WITH SMOKED SALMON & NOILLY PRAT

Noilly Prat is my favourite vermouth – for drinking and for cooking – as it has a real clarity and freshness of flavour. This is a typical meal-in-a-rush dish for those who have a large supermarket nearby.

Serves 4

500g fresh pasta of your choice
8–10 spring onions, trimmed and sliced
2 tbsp olive oil
2 fresh kaffir lime leaves (optional), finely shredded
1 lime, grated zest and juice
100ml/½ cup Noilly Prat
300ml/1¼ cups vegetable stock
6 tbsp crème fraîche
225g smoked salmon pieces
salt and freshly ground black pepper

1 Bring a large pan of salted water to the boil to cook the pasta. Meanwhile, cook the onions in the oil for 5 minutes in a large covered frying pan on the floor of the Roasting Oven. Add the kaffir lime leaves and lime juice to the onions, then add the Noilly Prat and stock and cook until slightly reduced on the Simmering Plate.

2 Cook the pasta in the boiling water for 4–5 minutes. Stir the crème fraîche into the sauce and cook until thickened, then add the smoked salmon, lime zest and seasonings to taste just as the pasta is cooked. *Just warm the salmon, do not really cook it or it can become slightly tough and almost ham-like.*

3 Drain the cooked pasta thoroughly, toss it into the sauce then serve immediately.

CREME FRAICHE

This is a soured cream from Normandy. It is thick, usually almost set, and has a slightly acidic taste which makes it an excellent seasoning for many foods. I often use it as almost a complete sauce as I like its tangy flavour, but many chefs would use it half and half with double or whipping cream. Crème fraîche has the added convenience of being a relatively long-life product.

Lamb & Rice Noodle Stir Fry

Noodles can be made from many different cereals and I have used the rice variety for this stir-fry as they are very quick to cook, and a little bit different. Use the Agaluxe wok or a heavy ground-based wok for this recipe.

1 Heat the wok on the floor of the Roasting Oven until required. Soak the rice noodles in boiling water for 5 minutes. Drain them and rinse thoroughly in cold water, then leave until required.

2 Add the oil to the wok, then stir-fry the lamb on the Boiling Plate for 3–4 minutes until well browned. Add all the vegetables except the bean sprouts. Continue stir-frying for 3–4 minutes, then add the bean sprouts, nuts, horseradish, mustard, ginger and salt or soy sauce to taste. Toss in the rice noodles with the hoi sin sauce, and cook for a further 1–2 minutes, until everything is piping hot. Serve immediately, garnished with the coriander.

Serves 4

3 tbsp chilli oil or sunflower oil
125g rice noodles
450g lamb neck fillet, trimmed and thinly sliced
6–8 spring onions, trimmed and sliced
1 red pepper, sliced
2 cloves garlic, crushed
125g baby sweetcorn, sliced
200g bean sprouts
50g macadamia nuts
1–2 tsp creamed horseradish
1–2 tsp French mustard or hot yellow English mustard
5cm piece fresh ginger root, grated and squeezed
salt or soy sauce to season
3–4 tbsp hoi sin sauce
2–3 tbsp coriander, freshly torn, to garnish

Pumpkin & Vegetable Lasagne

FOR TEN

It sounds very precise, but that's how it is! This recipe was developed one gloriously sunny Easter, when I wanted to be out in the garden and not indoors, cooking for a village party! I was on 'a large vegetable lasagne' duty, so I decided to allocate a 30–minute recipe test to the task. OK, it took 10 minutes to prepare and 30 more to cook, but I really felt that it was such a good, quick recipe that it had to be included!

1 large onion, roughly chopped
2 cloves garlic, roughly chopped
1–2 tbsp lovage or flat-leaf parsley, freshly chopped
2–3 tbsp basil, freshly torn
450g mushrooms
425g can pumpkin purée
400g can green lentils, drained
400g can chopped tomatoes
salt and freshly ground black pepper
150ml/⅔ cup water or stock
250g pack of 12 sheets fresh no-cook lasagne

Topping:

500g carton fromage frais
250g carton ricotta cheese
75g fresh Parmesan cheese, grated

Aga equipment:

small roasting tin on second set of runners in Roasting Oven

1 Lightly oil the roasting tin. Finely chop the onions, garlic, herbs and mushrooms together in the food processor – you may need to do this in two batches. Turn into a bowl and mix with the pumpkin, lentils, tomatoes and plenty of seasoning. Add up to 150ml/⅔ cup of water or stock to give a moist, slightly liquid mixture. The mixture needs to be moist so that the pasta doesn't become dry.

2 Layer the vegetables with the lasagne in three tiers – you will need to cut the fourth sheet of lasagne in half to fit the tin. Beat everything for the topping together until smooth, then add some seasonings and spread it over the lasagne. Bake for 30 minutes, until set and lightly browned.

Quick Puff Pastry Pizzas

A packet of ready-rolled puff pastry provides crispy bases for these pizzas, and the topping can be prepared while the pastry is cooking. They are light, stylish and delicious. The onion, pepper and tomatoes should all be cut into 6mm dice.

1 Unwrap the pastry and cut it into four circles, then mark a 1cm rim round each. Carefully brush the rim of the pastry with egg, then cook the bases on a baking sheet in the Roasting Oven for 12–15 minutes, until lightly golden.

2 Cook the pancetta and pine nuts in a frying pan on the Boiling Plate until the nuts are lightly toasted and the pancetta is starting to crisp. Chop the red onion, green pepper and tomatoes into 6mm dice and add them to the pan with the Gorgonzola and season well.

3 Carefully loosen the centres of the pastry cases, then press the circles down to make a thick base for the pizzas. Pile the vegetable mixture into the cases, then return them to the oven for a further 5–8 minutes, until the filling is just set. Serve immediately.

Serves 4

1 x 375g pack ready-rolled
   puff pastry
1 egg, beaten
70g pancetta
25g pine nuts
125g Gorgonzola or other
   sharp blue cheese, crumbled
½ red onion
1 green pepper, seeded
2 tomatoes, seeded
salt and freshly ground
   black pepper

Aga equipment:

wire shelf on third set of
   runners in Roasting Oven

Stuffed Chillies
WITH CHIVE NOODLES

Chilli mania is reaching the UK, and there is now a Chilli Society as well as various hot events up and down the country. At West Dean Gardens, near Chichester, 60 to 70 varieties of chillies are grown every year in a display glasshouse, and the plants are absolutely beautiful. Not all chillies are hot – the Anaheim variety used here is only slightly warmer than the regular green pepper, and they are widely available in season in major supermarkets. If you grow Hungarian Wax chillies, they can be stuffed in the same way.

Serves 2

2 large Anaheim chillies, halved and seeded

Filling:

6 spring onions, trimmed and finely chopped
75g blue cheese such as Blue d'Auvergne or mild Stilton, crumbled
8 tbsp fresh wholewheat breadcrumbs
25g pine nuts
2 tomatoes, seeded and chopped
1 tbsp cream (optional)
salt and freshly ground black pepper

Noodles:

1 sheet thread egg noodles (from a 250g packet of dried noodles)
1 tbsp olive oil
salt and freshly ground black pepper
2 tbsp freshly snipped chives

Aga equipment:

wire shelf on second set of runners in Roasting Oven

1 Halve the chillies and carefully remove the seeds. *Try to keep the tops of the cores intact as they will help to hold the shape of the chillies during baking.*

2 Mix all of the ingredients together for the filling, pack it into the chillies and put them in a small baking tin. Cook for 15 minutes in the Roasting Oven, until the chillies are tender and the topping has browned.

3 Soak the noodles in boiling water for 3 minutes, then drain them thoroughly. Heat the oil in a pan, add the noodles and toss them in the oil until hot, then stir in a little salt and pepper with the chives.

4 Serve the roasted stuffed chillies on a bed of noodles on warmed plates.

Peppered Kidneys
WITH CREAM AND CORIANDER

I love kidneys, and I like them cooked so that they are still just slightly pink in the centre. To achieve the required results I cook this dish on top of the Aga, so that I can see exactly what is happening. The amount of paprika you use will depend on the strength of the pepper.

1 Core and chop the kidneys. Heat the oil in a large frying pan on the Boiling Plate, add the kidneys and cook quickly until browned on all sides. Transfer to the Simmering Plate, then add the paprika and nutmeg. Continue to cook for 4–5 minutes.

2 Stir the cream into the pan and heat gently while adding salt and pepper to taste. Stir in the coriander leaves, then serve the kidneys immediately – perhaps with a wedge of lime to squeeze over them – with rice or noodles.

Serves 3

500g lamb's kidneys,
3 tbsp olive oil
1–2 tsp paprika (see above)
freshly grated nutmeg
4–5 tbsp crème fraîche or
  double cream
salt and freshly ground
  black pepper
2 tbsp coriander leaves,
  roughly torn
lime wedges, to garnish
boiled rice or noodles,
  to serve

Roast Fillet of Salmon
WITH ASPARAGUS & MUSHROOM PASTA

This quick supper dish is sheer luxury – a real treat at the end of a tiring day.

1 Bring a large pan of salted water to the boil, then add the asparagus and blanch for 2 minutes. Remove the asparagus with a perforated spoon and plunge it into cold water.

2 Add the tagliatelle to the boiling asparagus water, stir and return to the boil. Transfer to the Simmering Plate and cook as directed on the packet – about 12 minutes for dried pasta or 5 minutes if you are using the fresh version.

Serves 2

100g asparagus tips, cut into
  10cm lengths
150g tagliatelle, fresh
  or dried
200g mixed mushrooms,
  thickly sliced
1 clove garlic, crushed
25g butter

3 Cook the mushrooms and garlic in the butter and oil in a shallow covered pan on the floor of the Roasting Oven for 10 minutes, then add the drained asparagus and cook for a further 2–3 minutes.

4 Melt an extra knob of butter in a small frying pan on the Boiling Plate, then add the salmon, skin side uppermost and cook for 1–2 minutes, until lightly browned. Flip the salmon over on to a buttered baking sheet and roast on the wire shelf in the Roasting Oven for 5–6 minutes, until just cooked.

1 tbsp olive oil
2 salmon fillets, each weighing about 150g
2 tbsp crème fraîche
1 tbsp chives, freshly chopped

Aga equipment:
wire shelf on second set of runners in Roasting Oven

4 Pour any juices from the mushrooms and fish into the pan in which the salmon was browned. Add the cream and heat gently, then season to taste and add the chives.

5 Mound the drained tagliatelle in the centre of two warmed serving plates, then spoon the asparagus and mushrooms round. Top the pasta with the salmon, then spoon the sauce over the fish and tagliatelle and serve immediately.

PASTA – DRIED VERSUS FRESH

There is nothing to compare to home-made pasta, which, using a pasta rolling machine, can easily be mixed, rolled and cooked in the same length of time as it takes to boil the water and cook dried pasta. However, there are days when you just don't feel like setting to and mixing from scratch, so I generally keep some dried pasta in the cupboard for convenience.

It really is worth spending a little extra on pasta and buying dried shapes which are made from an egg dough – the basic mix is just flour and eggs so a commercial product made without eggs is going to be lacking in flavour.

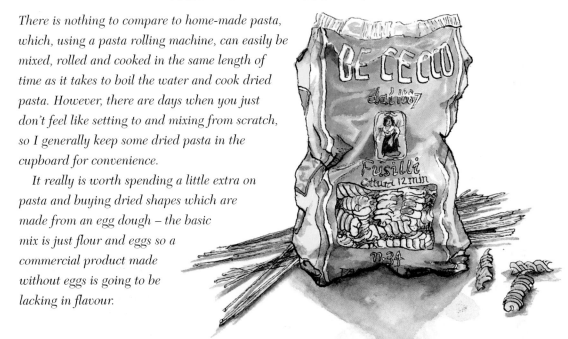

Fillet Steak Parcels
WITH RED WINE & KIDNEY GRAVY

The idea for this dish came from a friend's wedding one Christmas. The 160 guests were served a piping hot meal in a marquee in December, and it was a very good idea to serve fillet steaks in filo pastry – the browned steaks need only the quickest of cooking, until the pastry is crisp. I have added a wine and kidney gravy, so it is almost a contemporary steak and kidney pie!

1 Heat the butter and oil together in a frying pan on the Boiling Plate, then brush the filo pastry with a little of the mixture, stacking the sheets in pairs. Return the frying pan to the Aga, season the steaks and brown them quickly on all sides in the hot fat.

2 Spread the steaks with half the pesto, then wrap each one in pastry, gathering the corners up into a purse. Place the steaks on a buttered baking sheet and cook in the Roasting Oven for 10 minutes, until the pastry is crisp.

3 Meanwhile, add the shallot to the meat juices in the pan and fry on the Simmering Plate until soft. Add the diced kidney and cook quickly, until just starting to brown – *keep a little pink in the kidneys if possible*. Add the wine and cook rapidly until slightly reduced. Stir a further 1–2 tsp pesto into the sauce and season to taste.

4 Serve the steaks on a pool of the kidney gravy, with the vegetables of your choice.

Serves 2

25g butter
1 tsp oil
4 sheets filo pastry, about
    20cm/8 inches square
2 fillet steaks, each weighing
    about 125g
salt and freshly ground
    black pepper
2 tbsp red pesto or sun-dried
    tomato paste
1 shallot, finely chopped, or
    half a small onion
2 lamb's kidneys, cored and
    finely chopped
250ml/1 cup red wine, or
    wine and stock mixed

Aga equipment:

wire shelf on fourth set of
    runners in Roasting Oven

Mediterranean Roast Vegetables

WITH HARISSA COUSCOUS & LEAF SALAD

This is a complete meal in a salad. The cheese makes it quite a substantial main course, or you could serve it for a starter for 8.

Serves 4

1 small aubergine, trimmed
1 courgette, topped and tailed
1 medium red onion, peeled
1 red or orange pepper, halved and seeded
½ bulb of garlic, unpeeled
salt and freshly ground black pepper
olive oil
1 ripe but firm Marmande tomato, halved then cut into quarters
1 small head chicory, cut into 2cm slices
2 tsp harissa paste
250ml/1 cup vegetable stock
175g/1½ cups couscous
2 tbsp basil, freshly torn
100g chèvre or other firm goats' cheese, cut into small dice
salad leaves
2–3 tbsp vinaigrette dressing

Aga equipment:

large roasting tin on second set of runners in Roasting Oven

1 Cut the aubergine and courgette into 2.5cm chunks, then cut the onion and pepper into eight wedges. Place in the bottom of the roasting tin with the garlic and season lightly, then drizzle with olive oil and roast for 25 minutes, stirring and adding the tomato and sliced chicory after 15 minutes.

2 Blend the harissa and stock in a small pan and bring to the boil. Shoot in the couscous, stir then cover the pan and leave to stand on the back of the Aga until required.

3 Cut the skin from the roasted garlic and squeeze out the softened flesh, mixing it back into the vegetables with the basil and cheese and stirring until the cheese has melted. Fluff up the couscous with a fork, then divide it between four warmed plates. Top with the roasted vegetables and then a mound of dressed salad leaves. Serve immediately.

HARISSA

This is a blend of chillis and tomatoes originating from North Africa. It is usually sold as a paste in a tube or jar. As with all pepper sauces it can be explosively hot, so go easy with it until you are better acquainted! Harissa is particularly good with grains, and I often use it with couscous, cracked wheat or rice.

Spaghetti Carbonara

One of the most popular of all pasta dishes, this is little more than bacon and egg with some pasta thrown in. Mind you, I'd never say that to an Italian!

1 Bring a large pan of salted water to the boil. Add the pasta, then return it to the boil and cook for 10 minutes, or as directed on the packet.

2 Cook the bacon in the olive oil for 2–3 minutes in a large pan on the Simmering Plate – the bacon should not be allowed to brown. Beat the eggs with the cream, garlic and a little seasoning, then pour the mixture over the bacon in the pan. Cook slowly, drawing the pan slightly off the plate if necessary, until the egg is starting to thicken.

3 Drain the spaghetti, then stir it directly into the egg mixture. The heat left in the spaghetti should be sufficient to finish cooking the sauce. Add extra seasoning if necessary, then stir in the parsley and serve immediately topped with the shavings of Parmesan cheese.

Serves 4

300–350g spaghetti, depending on appetites
12 thin rashers smoked streaky bacon, chopped
2 tbsp olive oil
4 large eggs, beaten
150ml/⅔ cup single cream
1–2 cloves garlic, crushed
salt and freshly ground black pepper
1–2 tbsp flat-leaf parsley, freshly chopped
shavings of fresh Parmesan, to serve

Tex-Mex Tortilla Omelette

A quick, light omelette with lots of spicy flavour. I top it with a generous dollop of soured cream, or spicy tomato salsa, or both! Or you could use a spoonful of coleslaw. Some tortilla chips and guacamole might also be good on the side.

1 Heat a large non-stick frying pan on the floor of the Roasting Oven while preparing the potatoes. Peel then cut them into 1cm dice. Add the potatoes with the oil and chilli powder to the pan, stir well, then cover the pan and cook for 10 minutes on the floor of the Roasting Oven while preparing the other ingredients.

2 Add the remaining vegetables, stir well, then cook, covered again, for a further 5 minutes.

Serves 4

3 tbsp groundnut oil
2 large potatoes, weighing about 500g
1–2 tsp chilli powder
1 bunch spring onions, trimmed and cut into 1cm slices
1 red pepper, seeded and cut into 1cm dice

1 green pepper, seeded and cut into 1cm dice
1 clove garlic, crushed
6 large eggs, beaten
salt and freshly ground black pepper
2 tbsp coriander, freshly chopped

Aga equipment:

wire shelf on second set of runners in Roasting Oven

3 Season the beaten eggs, then stir them into the hot vegetable mixture. Cook, this time uncovered, for 5 minutes on the floor of the oven, until starting to set. Move the pan up on to the wire shelf and cook for a further 5 minutes, or until the omelette is completely set and slightly browned on top.

4 Serve cut into wedges, scattered with the coriander and topped with dollops of soured cream or spicy tomato salsa.

Chicken Fajitas
WITH HOME-MADE GUACAMOLE

Most Mexican food is quick to prepare. Fajitas are usually served 'sizzling' on an iron dish – heat it on the floor of the roasting oven if you have one.

Serves 4

2 tbsp oil
500g chicken stir-fry pieces or boneless breast fillets
1 tsp mild chilli powder
½ tsp ground cumin
1 green and 1 red pepper, seeded and roughly chopped
1 onion, cut into large wedges
juice of 1 lime
8 flour tortillas

Guacamole:

2 tomatoes
1–2 fresh red chillies
1–2 cloves garlic
2 spring onions
1 large or 2 medium firm but ripe avocados
1 lime, grated zest and juice
salt and freshly ground black pepper

Aga equipment:

wire shelf on third set of runners in Roasting Oven

1 First prepare the guacamole. Seed and finely chop the tomatoes and red chillies. Crush the garlic and finely chop the spring onions Roughly mash together with the other ingredients using a fork. Spoon into a serving dish.

2 Heat the oil in a large frying pan on the floor of the Roasting Oven while preparing the chicken. If you are using the boneless breast fillets, skin them and cut them into strips. Toss the meat in the spices, then stir into the oil and cook for 10 minutes on the floor of the oven, stirring once.

3 Stir in the peppers and onions and cook for a further 5–8 minutes, until the chicken is cooked through and tender. Wrap the tortillas in foil and warm them through on the shelf in the Roasting Oven when you add the peppers to the chicken.

4 Squeeze the lime juice over the chicken, then serve some in each warmed tortilla, topped with a dollop of guacamole.

Fruits de Mer
WITH FENNEL AND CREAM

For this I use a bag of frozen mixed luxury seafood – mussels, king prawns, tiny scallops and squid rings – so it is almost store-cupboard cookery. Use chicory, onions or peppers if you don't like fennel, but the mildly aniseed flavour of fennel is a good seasoning for the fish.

1 Cook the fennel and chillies with the garlic in the oil for 10 minutes – use a large covered frying pan on the floor of the Roasting Oven.

2 Transfer the pan to the Simmering Plate, add the seafood and stir-fry for 3–4 minutes – *the prawns in luxury seafood are often raw and blue-grey in colour, and they are cooked when they turn the more familiar pink.*

3 Stir the Noilly Prat into the pan and cook for a minute or so, then add the cream. Heat for just one or two minutes longer, until the cream is hot and just coming to the boil. Season to taste and add the coriander, then serve immediately while everything is still piping hot. Serve with freshly cooked vegetables or a salad and crusty bread, to mop up the juices.

Serves 2–3

1 bulb of fennel, trimmed and finely chopped
1–2 red chillies, seeded and finely chopped
1 clove garlic, crushed
2 tbsp olive oil
400g mixed luxury seafood, defrosted if previously frozen
1–2 tbsp Noilly Prat
4–5 tbsp crème fraîche or double cream
salt and freshly ground black pepper
1–2 tbsp coriander, freshly chopped

Quick Chicken Jalfrezi

This is a quick, stir-fried curry that can be cooked on the Aga plates, or on the floor of the Roasting Oven if the Aga is working hard and cooking other dishes at the same time.

1 Heat the ghee in a large frying pan on the Simmering Plate, then add the cumin seeds and fry them for about 1 minute. Stir in the garlic and ginger and cook for just a few seconds, until starting to turn golden, then stir in the chicken. Continue to cook on the plate, or the floor of the Roasting Oven, for 8–10 minutes, until the chicken is browned and almost cooked.

Serves 4–6

3 tbsp ghee
2 tsp cumin seeds
3 large plump cloves garlic, finely sliced
1 tbsp finely chopped fresh ginger root

700g diced boneless chicken – use breast meat or thighs, or a mixture of both
1 fresh green chilli, finely chopped
1 large onion, finely chopped
½ tsp turmeric
1 tsp mild chilli powder
2 tsp garam masala
2 green peppers, seeded and roughly chopped
3 tomatoes, seeded and chopped
2 tbsp coriander leaves, roughly torn
salt to taste
lime wedges, to serve

2 Use a perforated spoon to scoop the chicken out of the pan. Keep it warm on a plate in the Simmering Oven. Add the chilli, onion and all the remaining spices to the juices in the pan and cook for 5 minutes, until the onion is just soft. Cook on the Simmering Plate or the floor of the Roasting Oven – whichever you have been using.

3 Add the peppers and cook for 2–3 minutes. Return the chicken to the pan with the tomatoes and cook for 2–3 minutes. Season to taste with salt, then add the coriander leaves just before serving with wedges of fresh lime to squeeze over the jalfrezi.

Stir-Fried Beef
WITH CHILLIES AND GALANGAL

A Singapore-inspired dish. The galangal root is rather important – well, it's a main ingredient – but you could use ginger root which will result in a milder-flavoured dish. This is a dish to cook when the Aga is all fired up and you do not have to worry about conserving the stored heat for other dishes.

Serves 4–6
2 tbsp groundnut oil
1 large onion, thinly sliced
2 large plump cloves garlic, finely sliced
2.5cm piece galangal root, peeled and finely sliced
500g fillet steak, thinly sliced
1 tbsp dark soy sauce
1 tbsp fish sauce
1 tbsp yellow bean sauce or paste (paste is better if you can get it)
100ml/½cup well-flavoured beef stock
1–2 tsp demerara sugar
1–2 red chillies

1 Heat a wok or large frying pan for 5 minutes on the floor of the Roasting Oven, then put it on the Boiling Plate and add the oil. Shoot in the onions, garlic and galangal root and stir-fry quickly until golden brown. Add the beef a little at a time so that the wok doesn't lose its heat, and cook quickly until browned.

2 Blend the three sauces together with the stock and 1 teaspoon of sugar, then add the chillies. Pour the mixture into the wok and cook quickly for 1–2 minutes. Season with a little more sugar if necessary, then serve immediately.

Potato Gnocchi
WITH QUICK TOMATO SAUCE

Best described as little Italian potato dumplings, gnocchi are now available from supermarkets and grocers. They may be boiled and then served with just butter and Parmesan, but that always seems utterly decadent to me. I opt for a quick tomato sauce, a recipe which can be used with any number of dishes.

1 Bring a large pan of salted water to the boil. Meanwhile, cook the onion and garlic in the oil in a covered pan on the floor of the Roasting Oven for 5 minutes. Stir in the tomatoes and continue to cook, uncovered, on the floor of the oven for at least 10 minutes or until required.

2 Add the gnocchi to the boiling water, bring back to the boil and cook for 2–3 minutes, or as directed on the packet – the gnocchi are ready when they float to the top of the pan. Drain well, then return to the pan. Add the butter and toss the gnocchi around until well coated.

3 Season the tomato sauce to taste, then add the herbs. Serve the gnocchi on warmed serving plates with the sauce spooned over, topped with Parmesan.

Serves 3

400g prepared potato
   gnocchi
large knob of butter
freshly grated Parmesan,
   to serve

Sauce:

1 onion, finely chopped
1 large clove garlic, crushed
3 tbsp fruity olive oil
2 x 400g cans chopped
   tomatoes
salt and freshly ground
   black pepper
2 tbsp basil, roughly torn
1 tbsp parsley, freshly
   chopped

PARMESAN CHEESE

Gone are the days when Parmesan cheese meant dry scrapings out of a cardboard drum! The best Parmesan is that marked Reggiano, which must be at least two years old before it is ready for sale. The hard rind is stamped with the name and a series of black dots, proving the authenticity of this northern Italian, unpasteurised cow's milk cheese. There is no substitute for Parmesan – cheaper cheeses of this (grana) type exist, but their shallow flavours make them a false economy. Parmesan is usually grated, and a fine grate is better than coarse. However, many contemporary recipes call for a garnish of parings or shavings of Parmesan, which are best achieved with a potato peeler. The cheese stores well provided that it is carefully and tightly wrapped, either in plastic wrap or foil.

Baked Sweet Potatoes

WITH APPLE-CRUSTED PORK

Baked sweet potatoes are utterly delicious, especially if served with a spicy butter – I usually add a chilli butter, but fresh chilli, coriander and lemon grass (often sold together as fresh Thai herb mix), all very finely chopped, make a splendid Thai butter for potatoes or fish. Choose small potatoes which will cook quickly.

Serves 4

2–4 small sweet potatoes, each weighing about 200g
75–100g butter
3 fresh red chillies, seeded and very finely chopped
salt and freshly ground black pepper
1 small tart green eating apple such as Granny Smith, cored and grated
100g fresh white breadcrumbs
1 shallot, finely chopped
2 tbsp parsley, freshly chopped
4 pork chops, each weighing about 175g
2 tsp mild mustard such as Dijon, Honeycup or American Mild

Aga equipment:

wire shelf on third set of runners in Roasting Oven

1 Cut the sweet potatoes in half lengthways and place them on the shelf in the Roasting Oven. Bake for 30 minutes, until tender.

2 Beat 50g of the butter until soft, then add 1 or 2 chopped chillies to it with a little seasoning. Shape into a small log in a piece of plastic wrap, then chill until required. Heat the remaining butter until melted in a small pan on the back of the Aga.

3 Mix the apple, breadcrumbs, shallot and one of the chillies together, then add the parsley, and season with salt and pepper. Bind the mixture together with the remaining melted butter.

4 Season the chops lightly, then place on a baking sheet and smear them with mustard. Press the breadcrumb mixture into a thick crust on each chop, then bake on the shelf with the potatoes for 20 minutes. Check that the potatoes are not overcooking.

5 Score the potatoes and let a slice of the chilli butter melt into each one before serving with the chops.

Slow Starts – Quick Finishes

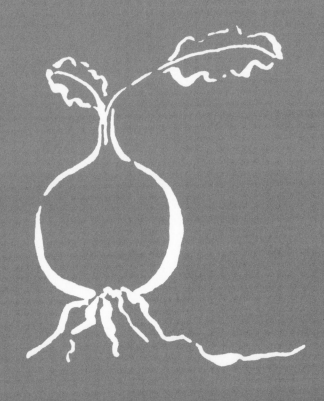

Mustard Braised Oxtail in Beer

WITH BROCCOLI & WALNUT NOODLES

I love oxtail, it's real rib-sticking comfort food. This is an ideal Aga dish – a long slow braise for the meat, and then a quick stir-fry of noodles and vegetables to finish. Of course, if you cook the oxtail the day before and refrigerate it overnight you will be able to spoon off any excess fat and the flavours will have a chance to blend together to an intoxicating infusion.

1 Smear the oxtail pieces with the mustard, then season them with black pepper and sprinkle with the flour.

2 Heat the lard in a heavy oven-to-hob casserole on the Boiling Plate, then add the oxtail and brown quickly on all sides. *Thorough browning is essential to the flavour of the finished dish.* Lift the meat from the pan with a perforated spoon.

3 Stir in the garlic and beer and bring quickly to the boil, stirring all the time to release any sediment from the bottom of the pan. Return the oxtail pieces with the seasonings, adding sufficient water to just cover the meat. Return the casserole to the boil, then cover the pan and cook on the floor of the Simmering Oven for 4 hours, or longer, until meltingly tender. Eight to ten hours cooking will not spoil the oxtail.

4 Heat a wok on the floor of the Roasting Oven for 5 minutes, then transfer it to the Boiling Plate and pour in the olive oil. Add the broccoli and stir-fry for 3–4 minutes until the broccoli is soft enough, especially if you have added the stalks chopped up (*this is a good idea as they have much of the flavour*). Move the wok to the Simmering Plate as the broccoli starts to soften or it will cook too quickly and burn.

5 Cover the noodles with boiling water and leave to stand for 5 minutes before draining thoroughly.

6 Remove the oxtail from the casserole and keep it warm on a plate in the Simmering Oven. Press the sauce through a fine sieve with

Serves 4

8 large pieces of oxtail, about 1.25kg in total
2–3 tbsp Dijon mustard
freshly ground black pepper
2 tbsp flour
1 tbsp lard or 1–2 tbsp vegetable oil (I think lard gives a better flavour)
2 large cloves garlic, halved
250ml/1 cup stout or bitter beer
2 bay leaves
1 cinnamon stick, broken
6 cloves
3–4 sprigs fresh thyme
450ml/2 cups water

Broccoli & walnut noodles

2 tbsp olive oil
340g broccoli, cut into tiny florets
250g packet medium egg noodles
75g/⅔ cup walnut pieces
1 clove garlic, crushed
1–2 tbsp walnut oil
salt and freshly ground black pepper
freshly chopped parsley, to serve

the back of a ladle into a clean pan and cook it quickly on the Boiling Plate until slightly reduced. Season to taste with salt, pepper and sugar, if necessary.

7 Add the walnuts to the broccoli and cook until hot, then stir in the garlic and drained noodles. Dress the stir-fry with the walnut oil, a little salt and pepper.

8 Mound the noodles on to warmed serving plates, then arrange the oxtail pieces on top and spoon the reduced sauce over. Garnish with plenty of freshly chopped parsley and serve immediately.

Bolognese Ragout

The first person I met who regarded the cooking of a Bolognese Sauce as a long, slow process was a transvestite male psychiatric night nurse who shared a cottage with a girl-friend and I many years ago in darkest Hampshire. The memory of his cooking lives on!

Serves 6

2 large onions, finely chopped
1 carrot, finely chopped
1 stick celery, finely chopped
3 tbsp olive oil
500g minced pork
500g minced beef
200g chicken livers, finely chopped
700g passata or chopped tomatoes
3 tbsp oregano, freshly chopped
2 bay leaves
salt and freshly ground black pepper
½ freshly grated nutmeg
2 cloves garlic, crushed
salad leaves, to garnish
fresh or dried pasta and freshly grated Parmesan, to serve

1 Cook the chopped onion, carrot and celery in the oil in a large covered oven-to-hob casserole on the floor of the Roasting Oven for 5–8 minutes.

2 Stir in the beef and pork, and cook quickly on the top of the Aga until the meats are browned – use the Simmering Plate if the Boiling Plate is too hot and the meat starts to stick. Shoot in the chicken livers and cook them very briefly, until just starting to brown, then add the passata, herbs, and salt and pepper with about half a nutmeg grated. Bring the ragout slowly to the boil, then cover the pan and cook on the floor of the Simmering Oven for at least 2 hours, but up to 8–10 hours is fine.

3 Bring a large pan of salted water to the boil, then add the pasta of your choice and cook as directed – about 10–12 minutes for dried pastas or 4–5 minutes for fresh. Drain the pasta thoroughly, then toss it into the sauce, seasoning well to taste. Serve with a salad garnish and freshly grated Parmesan.

Italian Beef

A gorgeously rich casserole of beef, cooked with plenty of my favourite Italian ingredients. An ideal dish for entertaining – easy to do and certain to impress.

1 Heat the oil and butter together in a large oven-to-hob casserole, then add the meat and brown quickly on both sides on the Boiling Plate – you may need to do this in two batches, and possibly to move the pan to the Simmering Plate if the other is too hot. Scoop the beef out of the casserole and set to one side.

2 Add the onions and garlic to the juices in the pan and cook, covered, on the floor of the Roasting Oven for 10 minutes. Pour in the vinegar and cook quickly on top of the Aga, stirring all the time to loosen any sediment stuck to the bottom of the pan. Add the passata, wine, oregano and plenty of seasoning, then bring to the boil. Bury the meat back in the pan, making sure that it is covered by the sauce and adding a little more wine or water if necessary. Cook on the floor of the Simmering Oven for 4–6 hours or longer: 8–10 hours will not harm the dish.

3 To serve: bring a large pan of salted water to the boil, then add the tagliatelle and cook for 4–5 minutes or as directed on the packet. Meanwhile, heat a wok or large frying pan on the floor of the Roasting Oven for 3–4 minutes, then transfer it to the Simmering Plate and add the oil. Add the leek and mushrooms once the oil is hot and stir-fry for 3–4 minutes without letting them burn.

4 Scoop the beef out of the sauce into a dish, and keep it warm in the Simmering Oven. Cook the sauce rapidly on the Boiling Plate until well reduced, then season it to taste.

5 Add all the other stir-fry ingredients to the leek and mushrooms. Drain the tagliatelle and add it to the vegetables then toss them together.

6 Make a bed of the stir-fry on each warmed serving plate, then top with a piece of beef and spoon the sauce over. Garnish with a topknot of rocket leaves and some shavings of Parmesan. Serve immediately.

Serves 8

3 tbsp fruity olive oil
knob of butter
8 pieces braising steak, each weighing about 175–200g
2 onions, finely sliced
2 cloves garlic, crushed
2 tbsp balsamic vinegar
680g jar of passata
350ml/1½ cups robust Italian red wine
1–2 tbsp oregano, freshly chopped
salt and freshly ground black pepper
rocket leaves and shavings of fresh Parmesan, to serve

Pasta:

225g fresh tagliatelle
2 tbsp fruity olive oil
1 large leek, trimmed and finely sliced
125g mushrooms, sliced
50g/½ cup pine nuts
1–2 cloves garlic, finely sliced
185g can pitted black olives, drained and sliced
4 halves sun-dried tomatoes, finely shredded

Wild Rice Casserole

WITH CAJUN SPICED CHICKEN

My friend Jane from Minnesota keeps me supplied with local wild rice. She is in crisis over this recipe as she says no Minnesotan would ever serve Cajun chicken, and therefore insists that I specify that the wild rice should be from Louisiana. I don't really understand why she is making so much fuss – after all, most wild rice now is cultivated, so how wild is it anyway?

Serves 4

1 large onion, finely sliced
1 leek, trimmed and sliced
2 sticks celery, trimmed and sliced
1 red chilli, seeded and finely chopped
2 cloves garlic, crushed
2–3 tbsp olive oil
175g/1 cup wild rice
125g mushrooms, chopped
350ml/2 cups well-flavoured vegetable stock
1 red pepper, seeded and chopped
50g/⅓ cup pumpkin seeds
50g/½ cup pecan nuts, roughly chopped
1–2 tbsp chives and parsley, mixed, freshly chopped
salt and freshly ground black pepper

Cajun chicken:

4 chicken breast fillets
1 lime, grated zest and juice
1 tbsp olive oil
1–2 tsp Cajun seasoning, according to taste
freshly chopped parsley, to garnish

1 Cook the onion, leek, celery, chilli and garlic in the oil in a large covered oven-to-hob casserole on the floor of the Roasting Oven for 10 minutes – the vegetables should just be starting to soften.

2 Stir in the rice, mushrooms and stock, then bring the mixture quickly to the boil. Cook, uncovered, on the Simmering Plate or the floor of the Roasting Oven for 10 minutes – *the rice must be simmering during this time.* Cover the casserole then cook on the floor of the Simmering Oven for 3 hours.

3 Marinade the chicken while the rice is cooking. Mix the lime zest and juice, the oil and Cajun seasoning together, then add the chicken breasts and turn them over in the mixture. Leave until ready to cook.

4 Check the rice – some of the grains should have burst and the casserole should have thickened. Stir in the red pepper, pumpkin seeds and pecans, then bring to the boil again. Cover and return to the floor of the Simmering Oven for up to a further 30 minutes.

5 Meanwhile, heat a grill pan on the floor of the Roasting Oven for 5 minutes, then add the chicken and sear it on each side, pressing down with a spatula. Transfer the grill pan to the floor of the Roasting Oven and cook for 12–15 minutes. Add any surplus marinade to the rice once you have seared the chicken.

6 Stir the mixed chives and parsley into the rice and season to taste. Serve each chicken breast on a mound of rice on warmed serving plates and spoon some of the juices from the rice over the chicken. Garnish with chopped parsley.

Slow Braised Shoulder of Lamb

WITH TWO-BEAN MASH, PRUNES
& WARM PROVENÇALE SALAD

Lamb and flageolet beans are such a classic combination that I was desperate to do something with them and yet be different. The result of my experimentation is a filling contemporary dish based on traditional ingredients. Very Lot valley!

1 Soak the beans for about 8 hours. Rinse both types of bean, then place them together in a pan of fresh water and bring quickly to the boil. Cook on the Simmering Plate maintaining a boil for 10 minutes, then transfer the covered pan to the floor of the Simmering Oven and cook the beans overnight or for 8 hours.

2 Drain the beans and reserve 200g for the stuffing. Place the remainder in the bottom of a suitable oven-to-hob casserole with the roughly chopped vegetables, 2 sprigs of the rosemary and 2 cloves of garlic, making a bed for braising the lamb.

3 Mix together all the ingredients for the stuffing, mashing the beans lightly as you go. Fill the blade bone cavity, then truss the opening with string to enclose the stuffing, or hold it closed with skewers or cocktail sticks. Add any extra stuffing to the mixture in the bottom of the casserole. Place the lamb on the beans, then make small slits all over the top of the joint with a sharp knife and fill them with slivers of the remaining garlic and tiny sprigs of rosemary. Pour the stock into the pan around the joint.

4 Open-roast the lamb for 30 minutes on the wire shelf in the Roasting Oven, then cover and transfer the casserole to the floor of the Simmering Oven for 2½–3 hours, until the meat is tender and cooked through. Take the meat from the casserole, place it in the roasting tin and crisp the fat in the Roasting Oven for 30 minutes. Leave it to stand for 15–20 minutes before carving.

Serves 6–8

150g/¾ cup flageolet beans, soaked and drained
100g/¾ cup cannellini beans, soaked and drained
1 onion, roughly chopped
1 carrot, roughly chopped
2 sticks celery, roughly chopped
3 sprigs rosemary
3 cloves garlic
1 shoulder of lamb, about 1.5kg, blade bone removed (this provides and ideal cavity for the stuffing)
salt and freshly ground black pepper
250ml/1 cup hot vegetable stock

Stuffing:

200g/1 cup cooked beans (see above and below!)
1 small onion, finely chopped
50g/½ cup walnut pieces, roughly chopped
100g prunes, pitted and chopped
salt and freshly ground black pepper

Provençale salad:

1 red onion, finely chopped
1 small aubergine, finely sliced

3 tbsp fruity olive oil
1 courgette, trimmed
and chopped
½ small red pepper, seeded
and chopped
½ small green pepper,
seeded and chopped

Aga equipment:

wire shelf on third set of
runners in Roasting Oven,
then small roasting tin on
third set of runners in
Roasting Oven

6 Drain as much of the juice from the beans as possible, then purée the beans and vegetables to a mash.

7 For the salad, cook the onion and aubergine in the oil in a covered pan for 10 minutes on the floor of the Roasting Oven. Add the remaining vegetables, and bring to the boil on the Simmering Plate and season well. Cover the pan and leave on the back of the Aga until required.

8 Carve the lamb in thick slices. Arrange the meat on a bed of the bean mash and spoon the salad vegetables round. Spoon any juices left in the roasting tin over the lamb with the vegetable juices.

Singapore Chicken Curry

A fragrant, mild curry which is full of big coconut flavour. There's no typing error in the amount of coconut powder needed for this dish. Serve with naan bread or chapatis and a small salad.

Serves 4–6
500g boneless chicken
(breasts or thighs, or a
mixture of the two), diced
2 tbsp medium curry paste
3 tbsp oil
4 tomatoes, quartered
1 small green pepper, seeded
and diced
125g/1 cup coconut powder
100ml/½ cup water
1 tsp salt
250g runner beans, stringed
and sliced
salad leaves, to garnish

Rempah:

1 large onion, roughly chopped
4 cloves garlic, roughly chopped
5cm piece fresh ginger root,
peeled and roughly chopped

1 Toss the diced chicken with the curry paste until all the pieces are evenly coated, then leave to marinade whilst preparing the other ingredients.

2 Roughly chop all the ingredients for the rempah together in a food processor – do not blend to a paste but keep some texture. Heat the oil in an oven-to-hob casserole then add the rempah and brown it quickly on the Boiling Plate. Stir in the chicken and cook for a minute or so, until lightly browned. Stir in the tomatoes, pepper and coconut powder, then add the water and salt and bring to the boil. Stir well, then cover the pan and transfer it to the floor of the Simmering Oven for 3 hours, or until the chicken is meltingly tender.

3 Just before serving, heat a little oil in a wok and stir-fry the runner beans, or simmer them for just 3–4 minutes then drain. Stir the beans into the curry, then season to taste and serve with warm breads and a salad garnish.

Turkey Buco
WITH RISOTTO MILANESE

So many people now don't eat veal, and yet the classic dish of tomato-braised veal served with saffron rice is too good to give up. Turkey leg steaks, which are available in most supermarkets, offer a good alternative to the traditional meat.

1 Heat the oil in a large oven-to-hob casserole on the Boiling Plate, then add the turkey and brown on both sides. Transfer the turkey to a plate, then toss the prepared vegetables and bacon in the juices in the pan. Cover and cook on the floor of the Roasting Oven for 10 minutes.

2 Add the wine to the vegetables, then cook, uncovered, on the Boiling Plate for 3–4 minutes, until the wine has reduced by about half. Add all the remaining ingredients for the casserole and bring to the boil. Return the turkey to the pan then cover and cook on the floor of the Simmering Oven for 3–4 hours.

3 About 45 minutes before serving you need to prepare the risotto. Steep the saffron in the boiling vegetable stock. Melt the butter into the oil in a large frying pan on the floor of the Roasting Oven, then add the onion, cover and cook for 10 minutes. Stir in the rice and cook on the Simmering Plate for a minute or so, then add the saffron stock, wine, garlic and a pinch of salt. Bring to the boil, then cook uncovered on the floor of the Roasting Oven for 20–25 minutes until the rice is soft and creamy, stirring once. Add the cheese and extra butter, then season to taste.

4 Mix together all the ingredients for the garnish. Serve the turkey on a bed of risotto with plenty of the vegetables and tomato sauce spooned over. Sprinkle each serving with the lemon and garlic garnish. *You should not need to reduce the turkey sauce before serving but, if it is necessary, keep the turkey warm in the Simmering Oven while boiling the sauce quickly on top of the Aga.*

Serves 4

3 tbsp fruity olive oil
4 turkey leg steaks or chops,
  each weighing about 125g
1 large onion, finely chopped
2 stalks celery, chopped
1 carrot, finely diced
1–2 rashers streaky bacon or
  pancetta, chopped
300ml/1¼ cups dry white wine,
  or wine and stock mixed
6 halves sun-dried tomatoes,
  shredded
2 cloves garlic, finely sliced
400g can chopped tomatoes
2 tbsp basil, freshly torn
1–2 tbsp oregano, freshly
  chopped
salt and freshly ground
  black pepper
1 clove garlic, finely chopped,
  pared zest of 1 lemon, and
  1 tbsp parsley, freshly
  chopped, to garnish

Risotto:
good pinch of saffron strands
900ml/4 cups vegetable stock
25g butter
2 tbsp fruity olive oil
1 large onion, finely chopped
200g/1 cup risotto rice
250ml/1 cup dry white wine
2 cloves garlic, crushed
salt
75g Parmesan, freshly grated
25g butter, in slivers
freshly ground black pepper

Pork Goulash
WITH PARSLEY & CARAWAY DUMPLINGS

If you can find a butcher who will sell you boneless spare rib for this goulash, you will certainly have a memorable feast.

Serves 4

2 tbsp olive oil
500g pork leg steaks or boneless spare rib, diced
125g smoked streaky bacon, rind removed and diced
2 large onions, chopped
2 peppers, seeded and chopped
2 cloves garlic, crushed or sliced
3 stalks celery, sliced
1 tsp caraway seeds
2 tbsp Hungarian hot paprika (Spanish paprika tends to be too sweet for this)
1–2 tbsp tarragon, freshly chopped
400g can chopped tomatoes
250ml/1 cup vegetable or chicken stock
salt and freshly ground black pepper
demerara sugar (optional)
4–5 tbsp crème fraîche
2–3 tbsp chives, freshly chopped
stir-fried green vegetables, to serve

Dumplings:

125g/1 cup self-raising flour
½ tsp salt
1 tsp caraway seeds
2 tbsp parsley, freshly chopped
75g/⅓ cup shredded suet
cold water

1 Heat the oil in an oven-to-hob casserole on the Boiling Plate, then add the pork and brown it on all sides, moving the pan across to the Simmering Plate if necessary. Scoop out the meat on to a plate using a perforated spoon, then add the bacon, vegetables, caraway and paprika to the meat juices and stir well. Cover the pan and cook on the floor of the Roasting Oven for 10–15 minutes, until everything has softened.

2 Stir the pork back into the casserole with the tarragon and tomatoes, the stock and a little seasoning. Bring to the boil, then cover and transfer to the floor of the Simmering Oven to cook for at least 4 hours and up to 6–8 hours.

3 Mix all the ingredients for the dumplings then bind them lightly into a soft dough with cold water. Just toss the dough in flour on the work surface so that it doesn't stick to your hands, then break off walnut sized pieces to make 12 rough dumplings, rolling them briefly – *they don't have to be perfect rounds.*

4 Remove the goulash from the oven to the Simmering Plate. Season to taste with extra salt and pepper, and a little demerara sugar, if required, then drop in the dumplings once the casserole is at a simmer again. Cover and cook for a further 20 minutes on the floor of the Roasting Oven, until the dumplings are well risen.

5 Beat together the crème fraîche, chives and a little seasoning while the dumplings are cooking.

6 To serve: stir-fry the green vegetable of your choice – runner beans, courgettes, small florets of broccoli – until just tender, then arrange them on warmed serving plates. Nestle the dumplings into the beans, then top with generous ladles of the goulash, and a dollop of the crème fraîche.

Olive Daube
WITH CARROT & ORANGE PARSLEY PENNE

You have to go a long way to beat a good daube. I like to serve it with this unusual but highly complementary pasta.

1 Heat the oil in a large oven-to-hob casserole on the Boiling Plate, add the beef and brown it quickly on all sides. Scoop the beef on to a plate using a perforated spoon, then add the onion, bacon, carrots and celery to the juices left in the pan. Stir them round, then cover and cook on the floor of the Roasting Oven for 10 minutes.

2 Stir the vinegar and garlic into the pan, cooking for 1–2 minutes on the Simmering Plate until any sediment has been released from the bottom of the pan. Gradually add the red wine, then bring to the boil. Add just the zest of the orange and all the remaining ingredients except the olive paste and olives, then return the meat to the pan, making sure that it is covered by the wine. Once simmering, cover the pan and cook on the floor of the Simmering Oven for at least 4 hours, and up to 6–8 hours.

3 To prepare the penne, bring a large pan of salted water to the boil, then cook the pasta for 12–15 minutes, or as directed on the packet. Add the carrots to the pasta for the last 5 minutes of cooking. Drain well. Melt the butter in the pasta pan then add the orange juice (the zest went into the beef) and bring quickly to the boil, adding a little salt and pepper – add a little extra orange juice if necessary to make about 5 tablespoons of dressing. Return the pasta and carrots to the pan, toss them in the dressing, then quickly stir in the parsley.

4 Stir the olive paste into the daube then add the olives and season to taste. Mound the penne in warmed serving bowls and serve topped with the beef and plenty of the delicious sauce. Garnish each portion with a generous heap of watercress.

Serves 6–8

3 tbsp fruity olive oil
850g–1kg shin of beef or chuck steak, cut into 5cm pieces
2 onions, finely chopped
225g smoked back bacon, rind removed and chopped
2 carrots, thickly sliced
2 sticks celery, sliced
2 tbsp red wine vinegar
2 cloves garlic, finely sliced
1 bottle full-flavoured red wine
1 orange, grated zest and juice
50g/¼ cup Puy lentils
2 cinnamon sticks, broken
6 cloves
4 bay leaves
3 sprigs lemon thyme
2 tbsp sun-dried tomato paste, or tomato purée
3 tbsp black olive paste or tapenade
125g black or green olives, halved and pitted
salt and freshly ground black pepper
watercress, to garnish

Penne:

225g good quality dried penne
2 carrots, cut into matchsticks
25g butter
salt and freshly ground black pepper
3 tbsp parsley, freshly chopped

Irish Stew
WITH THYME & LEEKS

If you pass this recipe because it reminds you of school dinners you will never know what you are missing! I love all the flavours which are so prevalent in this book; lemon grass, garlic, lime leaves, spices and herbs, but the clarity of the simple flavours in Irish Stew is devastatingly memorable.

Serves 4–6

1kg stewing lamb – middle or neck chops for every day, or best end cutlets for posh
1 litre/4½ cups cold water
salt
450g potatoes, peeled and chopped into large pieces
3–4 large sprigs of thyme
10 shallots or baby onions
2 large carrots, thickly sliced
2 tbsp groundnut or sunflower oil
300ml/1¼ cups whipping or double cream
2 leeks, trimmed and thickly sliced
freshly ground black pepper
3 tbsp parsley, freshly chopped, to garnish

1 Place the lamb in a large heavy casserole, add the water and a pinch of salt and bring quickly to the boil. Skim off any scum, then add the potatoes and thyme. Return to the boil, then cover and cook on the floor of the Simmering Oven for 3–4 hours.

2 Cook the shallots and carrots in the hot oil in a wok until the shallots are just starting to brown, then add the leeks. Continue to stir-fry for 3–4 minutes, until the vegetables are just cooked but still very crisp.

3 Remove the casserole from the oven and spoon the meat and potatoes into the wok using a perforated spoon. Ladle in about half the cooking liquor, enough to make a good gravy (reserve the rest for stock or soup) then add the cream. Bring to a boil, season to taste then add the parsley just before serving. Pile into the centre of warmed serving plates – it's all you need.

WINES FOR COOKING

Whilst few of us would actually go to the lengths of buying an extra special wine for cooking, it is a false economy to buy the cheapest as a great deal of flavour will be added to a finished dish by the wine that you select to cook with. Most dishes calling for red require a robust, full-bodied wine whilst a dry white is generally more suitable for cooking than a sweeter variety. Of course, the cook is far more likely to enjoy the left-overs if the wine is of reasonable quality...

Oriental Beef
WITH STIR-FRIED VEGETABLES & NOODLES

This is a recipe which I often use for mid-week entertaining. The longer you cook the beef, the cheaper the cut you can use. For 3 hours in the Aga use a braising steak like blade bone or, if you plan to leave the beef in the Simmering Oven virtually all day, use shin of beef.

1 Heat the oil in an oven-to-hob casserole on the Boiling Plate, then add the beef and brown it quickly on both sides. Remove the meat from the pan, add the onions and cook them quickly until starting to brown. Return the beef with the spices then add the oyster sauce, mixed with sufficient water to cover the meat. Stir in the soy sauce.

2 Bring the casserole to the boil, then cover and place it on the floor of the Simmering Oven. Cook for 3–4 hours or longer, until very tender.

3 Prepare all the vegetables for the stir-fry, cutting them into large, evenly sized pieces that will stay crisp during cooking. Pour boiling water over the noodles in a bowl and leave to stand on the back of the Aga for 3–4 minutes, or as directed, stirring once or twice to separate the strands.

4 Heat a wok or a large frying pan for 5 minutes on the floor of the Roasting Oven, then transfer it to the Boiling Plate and add the sunflower oil – it should be very hot, almost smoking. Shoot in the vegetables and stir-fry for 2–3 minutes, until just starting to brown. Drain the noodles thoroughly and toss them in a little sesame oil, then add them to the vegetables, tossing them together.

5 Pile the vegetable noodles on to four large warmed plates. Season the beef, if necessary, then arrange the steaks on top of the noodles. Quickly strain the sauce from the beef through a sieve and cook it rapidly on the Boiling Plate to reduce and thicken it slightly, if necessary. Season to taste, then spoon a generous amount on to each plate. Garnish with the chopped coriander and serve immediately.

Serves 4

2 tbsp sunflower or
  groundnut oil
4 thick pieces of braising
  beef, each weighing about
  175–200g
1 large onion, cut into eight
  pieces
2 whole star anise
1 cinnamon stick, broken
4 cloves
125ml/½ cup oyster sauce
2 tbsp dark soy sauce,
  preferably mushroom soy
2 tbsp freshly chopped
  coriander, to garnish

Stir-fry:

2 red peppers
2 green peppers
1 onion, cut into 8
1–2 cloves garlic, sliced
250g packet thread egg
  noodles
boiling water
2 tbsp sunflower or
  groundnut oil
sesame oil

Sesame Chick Peas

WITH APRICOT & RED PEPPER COUSCOUS AND ORANGE SALSA

A creamy, nutty dish of chickpeas with two types of salad – a hot, fruity couscous, and a brightly flavoured orange salsa.

Serves 4

350g/1½ cups chickpeas, soaked overnight
2 large onions, finely sliced
3 tbsp good fruity olive oil
1 tbsp ground coriander
1 tsp ground cumin
1 tsp ground ginger
1 mild chilli, seeded and finely chopped
2–3 juicy cloves garlic, finely sliced
2 bay leaves
400g can chopped tomatoes
350ml/1½ cups well-flavoured vegetable stock
salt and freshly ground black pepper
2 tbsp/¼ cup tahini

Salsa:

1 tbsp sesame seeds
1 large orange, zest and chopped flesh
2–3 spring onions, trimmed and chopped
2 tomatoes, seeded and diced
¼ cucumber, diced
4 dried apricots, chopped
1 mild fresh chilli, finely chopped
2 tbsp freshly chopped mint
juice of half a lemon

Couscous:

450ml/2 cups hot vegetable stock
150g/1 cup couscous
salt and freshly ground black pepper
3 spring onions, chopped
1 red pepper, seeded
4 dried apricots
25g/¼ cup pistachio nuts, roughly chopped
olive oil

1 Drain and rinse the chickpeas. Cook the onions in the oil in a covered oven-to-hob casserole on the floor of the Roasting Oven for 10 minutes, until very soft. Add the spices, chilli, garlic and bay leaves, and cook for a further 2–3 minutes before stirring in the drained chickpeas.

2 Add the chopped tomatoes, stock and seasonings. Bring quickly to the boil on top of the Aga and continue cooking quickly for 5 minutes. Transfer the casserole to the floor of the Simmering Oven and cook for 2–3 hours, until the chickpeas are tender.

3 To make the salsa, heat a frying pan on the Boiling Plate until evenly hot, then add the sesame seeds and dry-fry until just starting to pop. Allow to cool, then mix with all the remaining salsa ingredients. Season to taste, then leave to stand until required.

4 Boil the hot stock in a saucepan, shoot in the couscous, cover and leave for 15–20 minutes on the back of the Aga, until all the stock has been absorbed. Season with salt and pepper, add the spring onions, finely sliced red pepper, apricots and nuts, then moisten with a little olive oil, if necessary.

5 Remove the bay leaves from the chickpeas, stir in the tahini and season to taste.

6 Serve the chickpeas on a bed of couscous, spooning a little of the tahini sauce over and topping with the salsa.

Ribs of Beef

WITH CREAMED HORSERADISH GRAVY & VEGETABLE SPAGHETTI

There's something about ribs of beef in our house – no matter how large the joint, there are never any left-overs after the first picking! This is Aga Roasting par excellence. I would recommend visiting a butcher for the beef as you need the joint chined with the strapline removed, but with the rib bones still in place. Otherwise, order in advance from your supermarket.

1 Blend together the basil, olive paste, sun-dried tomatoes, garlic and seasonings, either in a processor or with a pestle and mortar. Spread the mixture over the meat under the fat where the strapline has been removed, then tie the fat in place with kitchen string. Place the joint on the rack in the roasting tin. Cook for 45 minutes in the Roasting Oven, then transfer to the Simmering Oven for 3–4 hours.

2 Prepare the vegetables. Shred the leeks very finely lengthways with a sharp knife, and grate the carrots and celeriac finely in a food processor. Have a large pan of salted water sitting on the back of the Aga, heating up in readiness to blanch the vegetables.

3 Rest the beef on the rack for 20 minutes before carving. Brown a little flour in the juices left in the roasting tin on the Boiling Plate, then add the red wine and boil until reduced to the consistency of a thin gravy. Stir in the horseradish, then season to taste. Carve the beef as thinly as possible.

4 Boil the water for the vegetables, then blanch them for no more than 30 seconds. Drain immediately, then pile them into the centre of warmed serving plates. Arrange the beef in piles around the spaghetti, then spoon the sauce over. Garnish with slivers of fresh Parmesan and serve immediately.

Serves 6

2 tbsp fresh basil leaves
3 tbsp black olive paste
8 halves sun-dried tomatoes
1–2 cloves garlic
salt and freshly ground
   black pepper
2 ribs of beef, chined,
   weighing about 1.8–2kg
1 tbsp flour
250ml/1 cup red wine
   or stock
2 tsp creamed horseradish
Parmesan shavings, to
   garnish

Vegetable spaghetti:

2 large leeks, with as much
   green as possible, trimmed
2 large carrots, peeled
1 small celeriac, peeled

Aga equipment:

small roasting tin with low
   rack on third set of runners
   in Roasting Oven
then second set of runners in
   Simmering Oven

Four-Bean Chilli
WITH MEXICAN TOMATO SALSA

I always think that the best chilli con carne and minced beef sauces are achieved by a long, slow cook, although we often think of these dishes as a quick supper. The Aga simmers to perfection. Go out for the day and forget about the chilli – it will come to no harm if you are late home.

Serves 4

200g/1 cup mixed beans such as kidney beans, chickpeas, haricot beans and split peas, soaked overnight
2 onions, finely chopped
2 tbsp groundnut or olive oil
500g minced beef
1 clove garlic, crushed
1–2 tsp chilli powder, according to bravery
1 tbsp oregano, freshly chopped
1 cinnamon stick
2 bay leaves
400g can chopped tomatoes
salt and freshly ground black pepper
stock or water
garlic bread, to serve

Salsa:

2 tomatoes, seeded and chopped
1 avocado, chopped
4 spring onions, trimmed and finely chopped
1 lime, zest and juice

1 Drain and rinse the beans, then bring them to a rolling boil in a pan of fresh water on top of the Aga. Cook for 10 minutes on the Simmering Plate, then cover and transfer to the Simmering Oven until required.

2 Cook the onions slowly in the oil in a covered oven-to-hob casserole on the floor of the Roasting Oven for about 10 minutes to draw out their natural sweetness. Stir in the minced beef, garlic and chilli powder and cook for a further 10 minutes on the floor of the Roasting Oven.

3 Add the herbs, chopped tomatoes and seasonings, then stir in the drained beans and bring to the boil on top of the Aga, adding as much stock or water as necessary to just cover the meat and make a thick moist sauce – don't add too much as very little will be boiled away during cooking. Cover the pot and cook on the floor of the Simmering Oven for at least 2 hours and a maximum of 10. *The longer you leave it, the richer the chilli will be.*

4 Prepare the simple salsa by mixing the tomatoes, avocado and spring onions together with a little seasoning and the lime zest and juice. Wrap the garlic bread in foil and heat on a wire shelf in the Roasting Oven for 15 minutes, or as directed. Serve the chilli with garlic bread and a spoonful of the salsa.

Sweet Potato & Chick-Pea Curry

You might say that this is a bit of a cheat for a Slow Start – Quick Finish recipe, but all you have to do to serve the curry is heat through some naan breads and make a quick tomato and onion salad. The chickpeas may be replaced with diced chicken, if you prefer – brown the chicken before the sweet potato, then continue as suggested.

1 Blend together all the ingredients for the curry paste, except the ghee, until smooth, using a liquidiser or food processor. Scrape the paste into a large oven-to-hob casserole, add the ghee, butter or oil and cook, covered, on the floor of the Roasting Oven for 10 minutes.

2 Bring the chickpeas to the boil in a pan of fresh water, then cover them and cook on the Simmering Plate for 10 minutes. Leave on the back of the Aga until required.

3 Stir the sweet potato into the curry paste, then continue to cook in the Roasting Oven for 5 minutes. Drain the chickpeas and add them to the curry with the chopped tomatoes. Bring to the boil on top of the Aga, then cover the pan again and cook for 3½–4 hours on the floor of the Simmering Oven.

4 Layer the sliced tomatoes and red onion for the salad in a small dish with seasonings over each layer. Scatter with the spring onions, then squeeze the lime juice over the salad. Leave to stand for 10 minutes or so.

5 Season the curry to taste, then serve with the tomato salad and warm Indian breads.

Serves 6

200g/1 cup chickpeas, soaked overnight and drained
500g sweet potato, cut into 1cm dice
400g can chopped tomatoes
1–2 tbsp coriander, freshly chopped
warm Indian breads, to serve

Curry paste:

1 large onion, roughly chopped
3 cloves garlic, roughly chopped
2 fresh red chillies, seeded and chopped
1 tbsp curry paste, as mild or hot as you like
1 tbsp lime pickle
1–2 tsp demerara sugar
1 tsp salt
5cm piece fresh ginger root, peeled and roughly chopped
4 tbsp ghee, unsalted butter or groundnut oil

Tomato salad:

6 ripe tomatoes, cored and sliced
1 small red onion, finely sliced
salt and freshly ground black pepper
4 spring onions, trimmed and finely sliced
juice of ½ lime

Crispy Aromatic Duck

My Aga version of the dish that has been a Chinese favourite for centuries. Traditionally the duck is steamed before being deep-fried, but I think a slow steamy cook in the Aga followed by a quick crisp on the floor of the Roasting Oven works just as well. Many supermarkets now sell duckling pancakes (usually in the chiller, next to the duck) but I actually prefer to wrap the meat in lettuce leaves.

Serves 4

4 large duckling portions
1 iceberg lettuce
½ cucumber, peeled and cut into thin batons
1 bunch of spring onions, trimmed and finely shredded lengthways
plum sauce

Marinade:

3 tbsp dark soy sauce (the richer the better)
2 tbsp clear honey
3 tsp Chinese five-spice powder
5cm piece fresh ginger root, grated

Aga equipment:

small roasting tin, high rack

1 Mix together the ingredients for the marinade, squeezing the juice from the grated ginger into the mixture. Rub the marinade all over the duckling, then leave for 8 hours or overnight in a cool larder, or loosely wrapped in the refrigerator.

2 Place the duckling on the high rack in the small roasting tin, then pour about 1cm of boiling water into the bottom of the tin. Cover loosely with foil then cook on the floor of the Roasting Oven for 20 minutes. Transfer the tin to the floor of the Simmering Oven and cook for a further 3–3½ hours, until the meat is cooked through and tender, then leave until cold. *You can prepare the duck in advance to this stage if you wish.*

3 Carefully separate the lettuce leaves and wash them, then allow them to drain on kitchen paper – do not squeeze the leaves or break them as you want them to remain crispy. Arrange in a serving dish. Place the cucumber, onions and plum sauce in separate little serving bowls.

4 Heat the empty roasting tin on the floor of the Roasting Oven for 5 minutes, then add the duck and cook for 20–30 minutes until piping hot and crispy – turn the duck over once and add a little oil to the tin, but only if necessary. Scrape the meat from the bones using a couple of forks, then arrange the shreds on a warmed serving dish.

5 Allow your guests to assemble the duck themselves. Spread a lettuce leaf with a little plum sauce, then add cucumber and spring onions. Top with some shreds of duck, then roll the filling up in the lettuce to eat it. *Don't forget the finger bowls!*

SOY SAUCE

A traditional seasoning for Chinese foods which largely replaces salt, there are now at least three different types of soy sauce for sale in most supermarkets. Soy sauce is made from an extract of fermented soybeans, the best sauces resulting from a natural fermentation. Light soy is a general seasoning and should be used with fish, noodle dishes and for salad dressings. Dark soy is more robust, having undergone a longer fermentation and should be used with all meat dishes – it has a much richer flavour than light soy sauce. You may have to visit a Chinese supermarket to find mushroom soy sauce, but it is well worth the effort. It is just as cheap as the other varieties. Mushrooms are used extensively in Chinese cookery and an extract from them is added to soy sauce, giving an extra depth of colour and flavour. Mushroom soy should be used for meat marinades whenever possible.

PERI-PERI

This is a hot pepper sauce which should really be spelt and pronounced piri-piri! It comes from the Mozambican name for the African bird's eye chilli, used to pep up and spice the bland flavour of so many staple African foods. It is now available in specialist food stores and large supermarkets, and is an excellent store cupboard ingredient to enhance any dish that is not quite as exciting as you had hoped.

FRESH GINGER ROOT

This knobbly tuber is usually peeled, then finely chopped for use in countless spicy dishes. In the never-ending quest to be different, I often grate the ginger, skin as well, on a coarse grate, and then extract the juice from it for use in my recipes. Gather up the shreds, then squeeze them firmly to release all the fragrant juice – the fibrous shreds can then be thrown away.

Mussel, Pork & Red Kidney Bean Gumbo

Gumbo is an all-in-one dish from the American deep South. It is usually made with a mixture of meat and fish, and I have added some beans for even more texture and flavour. The essentials are okra (difficult but possible to grow in a greenhouse) and a spoonful of cooked rice to serve in each portion.

Serves 6–8

2 tbsp fruity olive oil
325g pork tenderloin, cut into medallions about 1cm thick
1 tsp mild chilli powder
1 large onion, chopped
4 stalks celery, chopped
2 cloves garlic, crushed
500g okra, trimmed and cut into 2cm slices
200g/1 cup red kidney beans, soaked overnight and drained
468g jar passata
225g cooked brown or white rice

Sauce:

50g butter
1 tsp mild chilli powder
1 tsp ground cumin
3–4 sprigs fresh thyme
50g flour
450ml/2 cups vegetable stock
salt and freshly ground black pepper
1–3 tsp peri-peri sauce, to taste (it's hot, so take care!)
450g green-lipped mussels on the half shell

Aga equipment:

wire shelf on third set of runners in Roasting Oven, at the end of cooking

1 Heat the oil in a large oven-to-hob casserole on top of the Aga. Toss the pork in the chilli then cook it quickly for 4–5 minutes until browned – transfer to the Simmering Plate if necessary. Add the onion, celery and garlic, then cover the pan and cook on the floor of the Roasting Oven for 10 minutes while preparing the okra.

2 Drain and rinse the kidney beans. Bring them to the boil in a pan of fresh water, then cook on the Simmering Plate for 10 minutes. *Leave the pan on the back of the Aga until required.*

3 Stir the okra into the pork with the passata, the drained kidney beans and a little seasoning. Bring to the boil on the top, then cover and cook on the floor of the Simmering Oven while preparing the sauce.

4 Melt the butter with the spices and thyme and cook gently for a few seconds on the top of the Aga. Stir in the flour, then cook on the simmering plate for 2–3 minutes. Gradually add the stock, off the heat, then bring the sauce to the boil, stirring until thickened. Season with salt and pepper and add the peri-peri sauce.

5 Stir the sauce into the pork and okra mixture. Heat on the Boiling Plate until really bubbling, then put the lid back on the pan and return it to the Simmering Oven for at least 4 hours, and up to 10 hours.

6 Stir the mussels into the gumbo then cook for 5 minutes after re-establishing the boil on the Simmering Plate. Heat the cooked rice for 10 minutes in a small covered dish in the Roasting Oven, then serve a spoonful in the centre of each helping of gumbo, which should be served in dished plates or bowls.

Aromatic Confit of Duck
WITH GINGER SHOESTRING NOODLES

I have always been put off making my own confit by images of vats of duck fat and a general aura of greasy stickiness! Well, this recipe dispels my fears and is also very straightforward to prepare.

1 Trim up the duck, removing any excess skin from the portions. Scrape any fat from the skin and chop it roughly. Place the fat in a small pan with any chicken fat that you may have, and the water. Bring to the boil, then cover and transfer to the floor of the Simmering Oven for 2 hours, until all the fat is clear.

2 Meanwhile marinade the duckling in a dish by scattering the spices evenly over the portions. Use just enough salt to give a good covering to the top surface of the duck, then leave until required.

3 Rinse the duck portions under cold running water to remove all the salt and spices, then pack them into the bottom of an oven-to-hob casserole which will just take them snuggly. Strain the fat over the duck, and add sufficient groundnut oil to cover the portions completely. Cover the pan and cook in the Roasting Oven for 20 minutes, then transfer to the floor of the Simmering Oven for a further 2 hours, or until the duckling is very tender but not falling off the bone. Leave to cool in the fat, either for a few hours or overnight.

4 Heat the small roasting tin on the floor of the Roasting Oven for 10 minutes. Remove the duckling from the fat and scrape off the excess. Place the portions skin side down in the hot tin and cook on the floor of the oven for 20–25 minutes, turning once. Strain off most off the fat when you turn the joints, but leave sufficient to keep the meat moist and to prevent it from sticking to the tin.

5 Meanwhile, cover the noodles with boiling water and leave them to stand for 5 minutes before draining. Measure 2 tablespoons of the drained duck fat into a pan, add the spring onions and cook them briefly. Add the vinegar then squeeze the juice from the ginger shreds into the pan. Season the dressing to taste, then leave the pan on the back of the Aga until required.

Serves 4

4 duckling leg portions
chicken fat
150ml/⅔ cup water
groundnut oil
½ x 125g packet thread egg
    noodles
1 bunch spring onions,
    trimmed and chopped
    (cut them on an angle for
    presentation)
1 tbsp white wine vinegar
5cm piece fresh ginger root,
    coarsely grated
fresh coriander and chives,
    to garnish

Marinade spices:

3 tbsp finely chopped fresh
    ginger root
2 large cloves garlic, crushed
1 tbsp star anise (I use the
    broken pieces that are
    always in the jar)
1 tsp ground white pepper
2–2½ tbsp coarse sea salt

6 Drain the noodles and make small piles of them on warmed serving plates. Top with the confit, then spoon the spring onions and dressing over. Garnish the duck with coriander leaves and some chives, stuck upright into the noodles, and serve immediately.

Lemon & Garlic Slow-Roasted Chicken

I often cook chicken with lemon and tarragon, but the flavour of this pungent herb is lost if the cooking period is too long. So, for slow Aga roasting, I use a mixture of lemon and garlic.

Serves 6

1 large chicken, weighing about 2.3kg
2 bulbs garlic
2 large lemons
salt and freshly ground black pepper
1 tbsp fruity olive oil
2 tbsp sunflower oil
2 x 300g packets mushroom or Italian-style stir-fry, or stir-fry vegetables of your own choice, finely shredded

Aga equipment:

small roasting tin on third set of runners in Roasting Oven, then second set of runners in Simmering Oven

1 Trim the leg tips and wing tips from the chicken, and remove any excess fat from the neck of the bird (keep the chicken fat if you are likely to make a confit in the next few days). Season the chicken inside and out.

2 Separate the garlic into cloves but do not bother to peel them. Place about two thirds of the cloves inside the chicken, and the rest in the bottom of the roasting tin, sitting the chicken on top of them. Pare the zest from the lemons and cover it in plastic wrap for later use as a garnish. Rub the juice into the chicken, inside and out, then rub the olive oil over the breast.

3 Roast the chicken quickly for 30 minutes, then transfer it to the Simmering Oven and cook for at least 4 hours. Stand for 10–15 minutes before carving or, if you have left the chicken for six hours or more, pulling the joints apart for serving.

4 Heat a wok or large frying pan for 5 minutes on the floor of the Roasting Oven while the chicken is standing. Transfer the wok to the boiling plate and add the sunflower oil. Stir-fry the vegetables in the oil for 3–4 minutes, then serve the chicken on the vegetables, or mixed in with them, if the meat has fallen off the bone.

Cassoulet

One of my favourite post-Christmas dishes, and a great way to use up the left-overs of the various cooked meats. It takes a long time to cook a good cassoulet, but it is really no trouble at all with an Aga. Pre-Aga I contented myself with beany stews, but they are nothing compared to the Real Thing. Soak the beans the day before you want to eat the cassoulet and cook them overnight.

1 Bring the beans to the boil in a pan of fresh water, then cover and cook them quickly for 10 minutes on the Simmering Plate. Drain off any excess water, leaving just sufficient to cover the beans, then cook them, covered, on the floor of the Simmering Oven overnight.

2 Cook the onions in the olive oil in a large covered oven-to-hob casserole on the floor of the Roasting Oven for 10 minutes. Stir in the garlic and cooked meat and season well. Cover the casserole and cook for a further 10 minutes in the Roasting Oven.

3 Make a layer of the chopped garlic sausage over the cooked meats, then scatter the parsley over and add the chopped tomatoes. Drain the beans, then spoon them into the casserole over the meats, seasoning well. Add just enough stock to reach about 1cm below the level of the beans, then bring the contents of the pan to the boil. Cover and cook on the floor of the Simmering Oven for 3 hours or longer, but do not allow the cassoulet to become dry.

4 Make a thick layer of the breadcrumbs over the top of the beans, then bake the cassoulet in the Roasting Oven for 30 minutes, until the breadcrumbs are crisp. Serve with a tossed green salad.

Serves 8

500g/2 cups haricot beans, soaked overnight and rinsed
2 large onions, sliced
4 tbsp fruity olive oil
2 cloves garlic, finely sliced
700g mixed cooked meats such as goose, turkey, ham, chicken and duck, roughly chopped
salt and freshly ground black pepper
250g French garlic sausage, diced (buy the sausage from a delicatessen in one piece, then dice it)
4–5 tbsp parsley, freshly chopped
400g can chopped tomatoes
450ml/2 cups well-flavoured game, chicken or vegetable stock
150g fresh wholewheat breadcrumbs
tossed green salad, to serve

Aga equipment:

depending on your casserole, wire shelf on floor or on fourth set of runners in Roasting Oven for finishing the cassoulet

OLIVE OILS

Olive oils range in price from the affordable to the extravagant and it isn't possible to tell whether a higher price will mean an oil that is any more to your liking than a cheaper variety. The oils to avoid are those that are blended, especially if the oil is from more than one country, as the flavour will not have the required clarity. Virgin and extra virgin oils have the lowest acidity and therefore the most distinctive flavours.

I like to keep two or three kinds of olive oil in the cupboard. I usually buy virgin oil for cooking and reserve extra virgin for dressings and for drizzling over finished dishes. Mechanised centrifugal pressing means that virgin oils are now affordable for almost every kitchen use. Spanish oils are often very fragrant and grassy, and I keep them for mildly flavoured dishes or salads which contain fruit – they are also quite remarkable over sliced oranges to serve as a dessert. My favourite oils for general cooking tend to be from Greece or Crete, and it is these that I describe as fruity.

Supermarkets and delicatessens sometimes organise olive oil tastings for clubs and groups. These make fascinating evenings and show just how much variety of flavour there is in olive oil.

SESAME OIL

A good toasted sesame oil is heavy, dark and fragrant and should be used as a seasoning, in the same way as salt and pepper, at the end of cooking. Occasionally a recipe will call for you to cook with it, but this is an extravagance, although such indulgences can be very enjoyable! However, you may care to use the lighter, less aromatic groundnut, sunflower or chilli-flavoured sunflower oils for any recipe which asks you to cook with sesame oil.

WALNUT AND HAZELNUT OILS

These oils, often from France, are luxurious condiments and make wonderful dressings for salads, noodles and steamed vegetables. They are, however, too strong for mayonnaise and should be added to foods only when their very distinctive flavour is required. All nut oils have a relatively short shelf life as they will easily become rancid. Buy them in small quantities and keep them in a dark cupboard or larder – leaving them out in a sunny kitchen for your friends to admire will certainly shorten their shelf life.

Main
Dishes

Lamb Korma
WITH SPICED RICE

A mild, creamy curry that is ideal for informal entertaining. The rice is fragrant, not hot.

1 Steep the saffron strands in the milk until required. Whizz the onions, garlic and ginger together to a fine purée in a food processor or blender.

2 Melt the ghee or butter in a heavy oven-to-hob casserole on top of the Aga, then add the lamb and cook quickly on the Boiling Plate until browned all over. Stir in the onion purée, garam masala and the saffron milk, then cook, covered, on the floor of the Roasting Oven for 10 minutes.

3 Stir in the cream, almonds, poppy seeds and salt. Bring slowly to the boil on the Simmering Plate, then cover and cook on the floor of the Simmering Oven for at least 3 hours.

4 Start the rice soon after the curry has gone into the Simmering Oven. Soak the grains in plenty of cold water for at least 30 minutes, then rinse them thoroughly in a sieve under cold water until the water runs clear.

5 Heat the ghee in a heavy oven-to-hob casserole that will fit into the Simmering Oven with the curry – this is where Agaluxe pans really come into their own. Add the spices and cook on the Simmering Plate until fragrant and just starting to pop. Stir in the rice, making sure that the grains are well coated in the fragrant ghee, then add the water and milk. Bring quickly to the boil, then cover with a tight fitting lid and cook on the Simmering Plate, without peeping in, for 8 minutes. Quickly check that the liquid is now just level with the top of the rice, then snap the lid back on and transfer the rice to the floor of the Simmering Oven with the curry. The rice will keep a perfect texture if cooked for between 1–1½ hours without being disturbed.

6 Fluff up the rice with a fork, and add seasonings as necessary to the rice and the lamb. Serve the rice topped with the lamb.

Serves 6–8

good pinch of saffron strands
150ml/⅔ cup milk
3 large onions, roughly chopped
6 cloves garlic, roughly chopped
5cm piece fresh ginger root, peeled and roughly chopped
3 tbsp ghee or unsalted butter
1kg boneless diced lamb
2 tbsp garam masala
300ml/1¼ cups whipping or double cream
3 tbsp ground almonds
2 tbsp blue poppy seeds
1 tsp salt

Spiced rice:

350g/2 cups Basmati rice
1 tbsp ghee
3 bay leaves
3–4 pieces cassia bark, or 2 cinnamon sticks
1 tsp fennel seeds
1 tsp green cardamoms
2 star anise
1 tsp cumin seeds
350ml/1½ cups water
350ml/1½ cups milk

Singapore Chicken
WITH LEMON GRASS & COCONUT MILK

Singapore-style cookery has been a new discovery for me, but it ties in with the flavours of the Pacific Rim which are now so popular. A rempah is a spicy mixture, rather like a curry paste. If you can't get fresh galangal root, use 1 teaspoon of dried or fresh ginger root – galangal is best described as a hot, sour ginger.

Serves 4

1 tbsp chilli oil or
groundnut oil
8 chicken thighs, trimmed
1 tsp ground turmeric
1 stalk lemon grass, bruised
and finely chopped
8 kaffir lime leaves
1 tbsp demerara sugar
250ml/1 cup coconut milk,
canned or made up with
2 tbsp coconut powder
salt and freshly ground
black pepper
noodles or stir-fried
vegetables, to serve

Rempah:

2–3 fresh red chillies, seeded
1 onion, roughly chopped
2 large plump cloves garlic
2 stalks lemon grass, bruised
and roughly chopped
2cm piece fresh galangal
root, peeled and
finely sliced
25g/¼ cup macadamia nuts
or blanched almonds
250ml/1 cup water

1 Whizz all the ingredients for the rempah together, adding just enough of the water to make a paste.

2 Heat the oil in a large oven-to-hob casserole, then add the chicken and quickly brown it on all sides – you will probably need to do this in two batches. Use the Simmering Plate if the Boiling Plate is too hot. Add the turmeric, tossing the chicken pieces in the oil as you return them to the pan so that they are all evenly coloured.

3 Stir in the rempah, the remaining water, the lemon grass, lime leaves and sugar. Bring to the boil, then cover and cook on the floor of the Simmering Oven for 2 hours, or until the chicken is cooked through and tender.

4 Stir the coconut milk into the chicken, then heat it slowly on the Simmering Plate. Add any seasonings that are necessary then serve, perhaps with noodles and stir-fried vegetables.

Roast Loin of Pork

WITH CIDER & MUSTARD GRAVY AND SWEET ROAST VEGETABLES

A loin of pork was the first joint that I roasted in my Aga – the crackling was perfect and the results have coloured my expectations of Aga roasts ever since. The constant available heat of the Aga is ideal for roasting vegetables – roast carrots and beetroots are so delicious!

1 Ask the butcher to cut through the chine bone for you, or to remove it completely. *This makes carving very much easier.* Place the pork, crackling side up, on the rack in the roasting tin and brush lightly with olive oil. Sprinkle with salt, rubbing it gently into the crackling, then roast for about 1 hour and 15 minutes (55 minutes per kilo).

2 Place a separate roasting tin on the floor of the roasting oven when the meat goes in, with 5–6 tablespoons oil in the bottom – enough to just cover the base of the pan. Turn the prepared vegetables over in the hot oil – the colour from the beetroot may bleed slightly on to the other vegetables, but they will all brown in the oven, so it doesn't matter. Roast on the floor of the oven for about 1 hour, turning once or twice.

3 Rest the pork for 15 minutes before carving, removing the rack from the tin. Place the roasting tin on the Boiling Plate, add the cider and stir. Cook until the liquid has reduced by half, stirring up any sediment from the bottom of the tin during cooking. Add the mustard, season to taste, then add the cream. Continue cooking for 1–2 minutes, then thin the gravy as required with one or two ladlefuls of vegetable water or stock. Check the seasoning once again.

4 Carve the pork into thin slices and serve with the crackling and root vegetables, spooning the cider and mustard gravy over the meat.

Serves 6

1.5kg loin of pork, chined and with the crackling deeply scored
olive oil
salt

Sweet roast vegetables:

5–6 tbsp olive oil or sunflower oil, according to taste
1.2kg mixed root vegetables such as parsnips, sweet potato, raw beetroot, carrots, celeriac, peeled and cut into 5cm chunks

Cider and mustard gravy:

250ml/1 cup dry cider
1–2 tbsp wholegrain mustard
salt and freshly ground black pepper
150ml/⅔ cup double cream
vegetable water or stock

Aga equipment:

small roasting tin with low rack on third set of runners in Roasting Oven

Savoy Cabbage, Parsnip & Goats' Cheese Roulade

Quick to make, you can style this vegetarian roulade in a very professional manner if you have the time to blanch a few cabbage leaves to lay over the pastry before piling the filling into the centre. Thus, once the roulade is rolled, cooked and cut, you will have a vibrantly green border to the filling. If there are plenty of tomatoes around, serve the roulade with the Roasted Tomato Coulis (page 36).

Serves 4–6

450g parsnips, cut into 6mm dice
2 medium carrots, cut into 6mm dice
1 large onion, finely chopped
50g butter
300g Savoy cabbage, finely shredded
150g soft goats' cheese, either plain or flavoured with herbs and/or garlic
salt and freshly ground black pepper
1 tsp caraway seeds
1 egg, beaten
375g packet ready-rolled puff pastry, or equivalent

Aga equipment:

wire shelf on fourth set of runners in Roasting Oven

1 Put the parsnips and carrots in a saucepan and just cover with salted water. Bring to the boil, then drain off most of the water, cover and cook on the floor of the Simmering Oven for 10 minutes, or until required.

2 Cook the onion in the butter in a large pan on the Simmering Plate until soft, then stir in the shredded cabbage and stir-fry until the cabbage is just wilted. Drain the root vegetables and add them with the cheese, seasonings and most of the beaten egg.

3 Fill the pastry with the vegetable mixture, then roll it up to make a short, fat roulade, sealing the edges with egg. Carefully transfer it to a baking sheet and brush with the remaining egg. Bake for 25–30 minutes, until golden brown. Serve sliced with a tomato sauce or Roasted Tomato Coulis.

Sweet Roasted Chicken

Sweet roasted chicken, with a slight kick which comes from the kaffir lime leaves! Sweet onions are mild and often white in colour – they roast very well in a selection of root vegetables.

1 Loosen the skin of the chicken over the breast and legs with your fingers. Insert the orange slices and pieces of lime leaves under the skin with the orange slices covering the lime leaves (to prevent the leaves from drying). Place the chicken in the roasting tin.

2 Cut the potatoes into large chunks then turn them and the onions in the oil. Arrange the vegetables around the chicken then season everything with salt and pepper. Pour the wine over the chicken, then cover the breast with a butter paper to prevent it from over-browning. Roast the chicken for 1 hour, or until the juices run clear, removing the butter paper after 20 minutes.

3 Wrap the chicken in foil and leave it to stand for about 20 minutes before carving. Meanwhile, drain the juices from the tin into a pan for the sauce, then continue to cook the vegetables in the bottom of the roasting tin on the floor of the oven for 20 minutes, until slightly crisp, turning once or twice. Remove the vegetables with a perforated spoon and keep them warm in the Simmering Oven.

4 Stir the cream into the meat juices in the pan, then bring to the boil on the Simmering Plate. Season to the sauce to taste and stir in the parsley.

5 Carve the chicken. Spoon the sauce over the slices and serve with the roasted potatoes and onions.

Serves 6

1 chicken, weighing about 1.5kg
1 medium orange, sliced
3–4 kaffir lime leaves (optional), torn in half
2 large sweet potatoes, weighing about 800g, peeled
2 sweet onions, cut into quarters with the root intact (this keeps them together for presentation of the finished dish)
3 tbsp olive oil
salt and freshly ground black pepper
350ml/1½ cups Sauternes or other sweet dessert wine
150ml/⅔ cup double cream
2–3 tbsp parsley, freshly chopped

Aga equipment:

small roasting tin on lowest set of runners in Roasting Oven

Greekily-Lemon Lamb

The Greeks are wonderful at cooking with lemons – most of us just think of them as a seasoning but they turn them into wonderful soups, puddings and countless other dishes. This is not a traditional Greek dish, as far as I know, but it certainly owes its creation to Greek inspiration. The lamb is coated with a tangy crust, Aga slow-roasted then served with a white wine gravy.

Serves 6

1 shoulder of lamb, weighing about 1.8–2kg
150ml/⅔ cup dry white wine
150ml/⅔ cup vegetable stock or water
1 tbsp whipping or double cream (optional)

Crust:

2 lemons, grated zest and juice
4–5 sprigs fresh thyme
1 tbsp rosemary, freshly chopped
1 tbsp oregano or parsley, freshly chopped
1–2 cloves garlic, crushed
salt and freshly ground black pepper
3 tbsp flour

Aga equipment:

large roasting tin with low rack on second set of runners in Roasting Oven, then second set of runners in Simmering Oven

1 Mix together all the ingredients for the crust. Place the lamb in the prepared roasting tin. Score the fat extravagantly with a sharp knife, taking care not to cut right down into the meat. Smear a little of the paste on to the underside of the shoulder, then turn the joint over and rub the remainder well into the fat.

2 Cook in the Roasting Oven for 30 minutes, and then for a further 2½ hours in the Simmering Oven, until the juices run clear. Stand the lamb for 20–30 minutes before carving.

3 To make the gravy, drain away any excess fat from the roasting tin, then add the wine and bring quickly to the boil, scraping up any sediment from the bottom of the pan. Cook until slightly reduced, then add the stock and boil for 1–2 minutes. Season the sauce to taste and add 1 tablespoon cream if you dare.

4 Carve the lamb into generous slices, and serve with the sauce spooned over.

Steak, Kidney & Mushroom Pudding

The biggest problem with steaming puddings on a conventional cooker is the amount of condensation produced in the kitchen. No such problems exist when cooking in the Simmering Oven of an Aga.

1 Mix the steak and kidneys with the mushrooms, onion, soy sauce and plenty of seasoning, but do not add the water.

2 Blend the flour, baking powder, salt and suet together, then mix with enough cold water to make a soft but manageable dough – the pastry should be soft but not too sticky. Knead lightly on a floured surface, then roll out two-thirds into a large circle, and use to line a greased 1 litre pudding basin. Pack the meat into the pastry, then add sufficient water to come almost to the top of the meat, but do not allow it to overflow.

3 Roll out the remaining pastry to a circle just large enough to cover the meat. Damp the edges of the pastry and seal them together, pinching the crust into an attractive edging. Make a small slit in the pastry lid with a sharp knife to allow the steam to escape during cooking.

4 Lay a sheet of greased greaseproof paper on top of a piece of foil and fold them together to form a pleat. Tie them securely over the pudding with string, with the foil on the outside.

5 Place the pudding in a suitable pan, adding sufficient boiling water to come half way up the pudding basin. Bring quickly to the boil, then cover the pan and place it on the floor of the Roasting Oven for 30 minutes. Transfer to the floor of the Simmering Oven and cook for at least 6 hours, and preferably 7–8 hours.

6 Serve in generous slices with freshly cooked vegetables and creamy mash.

Serves 6

700g chuck steak, cut into 2cm dice
225g lamb's kidneys, cut into 2cm dice
125g mushrooms, chopped
1 onion, finely chopped
1 tbsp mushroom soy sauce or 1 tsp Worcestershire sauce
salt and freshly ground black pepper
150ml/⅔ cup water (approximately)
selection of freshly cooked vegetables and creamy mashed potato, to serve

Suet crust pastry:

225g/1¾ cups plain flour
2 tsp baking powder
125g/½ cup shredded suet
½ tsp salt
cold water to mix

Spiced Pot Roast of Pork

This is a wonderful dish – cooking pork in milk is a traditional way of producing a tender casserole or pot roast, and the addition of the spices makes a subtly different dish. I recommend roast root vegetables to go with it.

Serves 4–6

25g butter
1 tbsp groundnut or sunflower oil
salt and freshly ground black pepper
1.5kg joint spare rib or boneless shoulder of pork
2 large onions, roughly chopped
2 cloves garlic, halved
3 large bay leaves
1 cinnamon stick, broken
6–8 cloves
2 tsp cardamom pods, lightly crushed
150ml/⅔ cup milk
3 tbsp calvados
3–4 tbsp crème fraîche or double cream

Aga equipment:

wire shelf on floor of Roasting Oven
wire shelf on floor of Simmering Oven

1 Choose a small casserole that will just take the pork and heat the butter and oil together in it on the Boiling Plate. Season the pork, then brown it all over in the hot fat – *if there is a reasonable piece of fat on the joint it may spatter a bit when that side is being browned.*

2 Squeeze the onions and garlic into the casserole down the sides of the pork, then add the spices and pour in the milk. Cover and cook in the Roasting Oven for 30 minutes, then transfer to the Simmering Oven for 4–5 hours, or until completely tender. Don't put the casserole on the floor of the oven as you don't want the milk to catch. *You also want an all round heat for pot-roasting.*

3 Strain the sauce from the pork and press it through a sieve to remove all the seasonings and vegetables. Boil the sauce quickly until reduced by about two-thirds, then add the calvados and cook for a further 1–2 minutes. Stir in the cream, then season to taste.

4 Carve the pork into rough slices, then serve with the sauce spooned over.

Roast Marinated Venison

WITH MIXED MUSHROOM RISOTTO

Inspired by a fungi foray in the New Forest which ended up at Le Poussin in Brockenhurst, a restaurant specialising in dishes with wild mushrooms in the season. There's really no need to carve the meltingly tender venison – you can just put it on a platter in the middle of the table and let people pull off chunks with a spoon and fork. I prefer to use a leg of venison on the bone as it will keep its shape better during cooking.

1 Mix all the ingredients for the marinade in a non-metallic bowl (*a metal bowl might taint the flavour of the finished dish – glass is best*). Then add the venison and leave in a cool place for at least 6 hours. Turn the joint over once during marinating.

2 Remove the joint, pat it dry then season well with salt and pepper – strain and reserve the marinade. Heat the butter and the remaining oil in a large oven-to-hob casserole on the Boiling Plate, then add the meat and seal it quickly on all sides. Transfer the venison to the rack in the roasting tin and cook in the Roasting Oven for 30 minutes – do not throw away the juices in the pan from browning the meat. Transfer the tin to the Simmering Oven and continue roasting for 4–5 hours, or until the meat is almost falling apart or off the bone.

3 To make the risotto, cook the onion and celery in the oil left in the casserole. Cover the pan and cook them for 5 minutes on the floor of the Roasting Oven. Drain the dried porcini, reserving the liquor. Roughly chop them, then add to the pan with the sliced mushrooms. Stir well, then cover and cook for a further 10 minutes in the Roasting Oven. Stir in the garlic and the rice and cook for 1–2 minutes on the Simmering Plate.

4 Add the reserved mushroom liquor to the strained marinade and make it up to 850ml/3¾ cups with stock, water or wine. Add the liquid to the pan and bring everything quickly to the boil. Cook the

Serves 8

1.8–2kg leg of venison, on the
  bone, or a boneless roasting
  joint of similar weight
salt and freshly ground
  black pepper
25g butter
3 tbsp olive oil
salad leaves, to garnish

Marinade:

1 onion, finely sliced
3 bay leaves
1 tbsp fresh mixed herbs
6 juniper berries
6 black peppercorns
3 tbsp olive oil
3 tbsp sherry vinegar
½ bottle robust red wine

Mixed mushroom risotto:

1 large onion, finely sliced
2–3 stalks celery, finely
  chopped
20g dried porcini, soaked in
  sherry
750g mixed fresh mushrooms,
  peeled if necessary
2–3 plump cloves garlic,
  crushed
500g/2½ cups risotto rice

100g freshly grated Parmesan
2–3 tbsp pesto or 1 tbsp
tapenade (optional)
salt and freshly ground
black pepper

Aga equipment:

small roasting tin with low rack on
third set of runners in Roasting
Oven, then second set of
runners in Simmering Oven

risotto on the floor of the Roasting Oven for 35–40 minutes, until the stock has been absorbed and the risotto is creamy. Stir once or twice, which will enable you to keep an eye on how the risotto is doing. Stir in the Parmesan and pesto, then season to taste.

5 Serve the venison on a bed of risotto, perhaps with a few salad leaves if you really feel you need add anything extra to this wonderful dish.

Bobotie

WITH HOT YELLOW RICE SALAD

A spicy Malay-inspired dish, a favourite recipe from South Africa. A brilliantly flavoured and brilliantly coloured alternative to lasagne for simple entertaining.

1 Cook the onions in the oil in a large frying pan on the floor of the Roasting Oven for about 5 minutes. Soak the bread in the milk until required. Add the curry paste and turmeric to the onion and cook for a further 1 minute, then add the minced beef and fry quickly on the Boiling Plate, until the meat has browned.

2 Squeeze the bread dry, reserving the milk, and crumble it into the meat off the heat. Stir in the lemon zest and juice, salt, pepper, sugar, raisins, chutney and 1 egg. Pack the meat mixture firmly into a suitable buttered dish, then bury the lime leaves in the mixture. Cover with foil, then bake in the Simmering Oven for 2½ hours.

3 Begin to prepare the rice salad just before the Bobotie is ready. Cook the spring onions in the oil in a covered pan for 5 minutes on the floor of the Roasting Oven, then stir in the turmeric and rice. Cook for 1–2 minutes on the Simmering Plate, then add the stock. Bring to the boil, then cover the pan. Leave to one side on the Simmering Plate while finishing the Bobotie.

4 Measure the reserved milk and make it up to 300ml/1¼ cups with a little extra, if necessary. Beat in the remaining egg. Scatter the almonds over the meat mixture, then pour the milk and egg mixture over. Transfer the bobotie to the Roasting Oven, insert the cold shelf and cook for a further 30 minutes, or cook in the centre of the four-oven Aga Baking Oven.

5 Remove the wire shelf from the Simmering Oven and cook the rice on the floor of the oven for 20 minutes, or until all the stock has been absorbed. Stand the rice for 5 minutes, then stir in the remaining salad vegetables with the dressing.

6 Serve the bobotie with the rice, a tomato salad and extra mango chutney.

Serves 6

2 large onions, finely chopped
3 tbsp groundnut oil
1 slice bread, about 1cm thick
250ml/1 cup milk
1 tbsp curry paste
1 tsp ground turmeric
800g finely minced beef
1 lemon, grated zest and juice
1 tsp salt
freshly ground black pepper
1 tbsp demerara sugar
75g/½ cup raisins
3 tbsp/⅓ cup mango chutney
2 eggs
6–8 kaffir lime leaves, broken
extra milk
50g/½ cup toasted flaked
  almonds
tomato salad and mango
  chutney, to serve

Yellow rice salad:

8 spring onions, chopped
2 tbsp oil
1 tsp ground turmeric
350g easy-cook long-grain rice
450ml/2 cups stock
1 carrot, peeled and very finely
  diced
1 head chicory, very finely sliced
1 stalk celery, very finely sliced
3 tbsp vinaigrette

Aga equipment:

wire shelf on floor of Simmering
  Oven then wire shelf on
  bottom set of runners in
  Roasting Oven with cold shelf
  on top set of runners

Thai Chicken

I tried this recipe out rather nervously on Mark and Clare, the children next door – their Mum says that they eat anything but I thought it might be too spicy. They loved it!

Serves 4

1 large chicken, jointed, or
8 chicken joints
2–3 tbsp coriander, freshly
chopped

Marinade:

2 limes, grated zest and juice
1 large piece fresh ginger
root, grated and the juice
squeezed from it
1 hot fresh red chilli such as
Bird's Eye, seeded and
roughly chopped
1 stalk lemon grass, bruised
and chopped
4 kaffir lime leaves
2 cloves garlic, crushed
½ tsp salt
freshly ground black pepper
3 tbsp groundnut oil or
chilli oil

1 Mix together all the ingredients for the marinade then add the chicken. Leave for at least 30 minutes, turning the chicken pieces over from time to time.

2 Heat a ridged grill pan on the floor of the Roasting Oven for 10 minutes. Shake the chicken pieces dry, then place them on the griddle and press down firmly to mark the meat. Cook for 10 minutes on the floor of the oven, then turn the joints over and cook for a further 15–20 minutes, until cooked through.

3 Serve garnished with the coriander. The marinade may be simmered for 5 minutes, then strained before being spooned over the chicken.

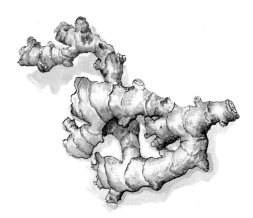

Greek Spinach & Feta Pie

Quick to make – as long as you remember to defrost the spinach – this is an excellent pie for informal entertaining at home, in the garden or on picnics. Do not cheat and leave the parsley out, it really makes a significant contribution to the seasoning of the spinach.

1 If you should forget to defrost the spinach, place it in a large covered pan on the floor of the Roasting Oven and cook for 20–25 minutes, stirring once or twice, until completely defrosted.

2 Place the spinach, Aga defrosted or otherwise, in a large pan on the Boiling Plate, and cook for 1–2 minutes, stirring and watching carefully, until all the surplus water is driven off – *keep stirring the spinach to prevent it from burning*. If the spinach just keeps making extra water, you may have to press it through a sieve or colander, but do strive to get it as dry as possible.

3 Allow the spinach to cool slightly, then mix it with the pine nuts, garlic, parsley, feta, nutmeg and seasoning, binding together with the beaten eggs.

4 Melt the butter, then brush it over the filo pastry. Line a deep 20–22.5cm ovenproof dish or baking tin with most of the pastry. Pack the spinach mixture into the pastry case, then top with the remaining sheets of filo, rolling the edges over to make a neat edge to the pie. Score the pastry topping into diamond shapes with a sharp, serrated knife, then bake the spinach pie on floor of the Roasting Oven for 30 minutes. Serve warm.

Serves 6

1kg frozen spinach, defrosted
50g/½ cup pine nuts
1–2 cloves garlic, crushed
2–3 tbsp parsley, freshly chopped
100g feta cheese, cut into small dice
freshly grated nutmeg
salt and freshly ground black pepper
2 large eggs, beaten
50g butter
10–15 sheets filo pastry, depending on size

Venison

WITH CHESTNUTS, ORANGE & JUNIPER

I have yet to come to terms with the desire to eat ostrich, buffalo and the other so called 'exotic' meats that are now on most supermarket shelves! We have our own very excellent alternative meat in venison, low in fat, high in flavour and very reasonably priced if you can find a good game butcher in the country.

Serves 6

1kg diced boneless forequarter of venison
1 large onion, finely chopped
6 rashers smoked streaky bacon, rind removed and chopped
25g butter
1 tbsp olive oil
10 juniper berries, lightly crushed
1 tbsp rosemary, freshly chopped
salt and freshly ground black pepper
350ml/1½ cups orange juice
150g button mushrooms
200g peeled chestnuts, fresh or vacuum packed
1 orange, to garnish
1–2 tbsp fragrant olive oil or sunflower oil
fresh rosemary sprigs, to garnish

Marinade:

1 large onion, sliced
1 clove garlic, sliced
10 juniper berries, lightly crushed
1 tsp black peppercorns
1 tsp salt
1 tbsp coriander seeds, lightly crushed
3 tbsp blackcurrant, raspberry or sherry vinegar
½ bottle robust red wine

1 Place the venison in a glass bowl and add all the ingredients for the marinade. Stir well, then cover and leave in a cool place for 6–8 hours or overnight. *Do not use a plastic or metallic bowl for marinating, as this may taint the flavour of the finished dish.*

2 Cook the onion and bacon with the butter and olive oil in a large covered oven-to-hob casserole on the floor of the Roasting Oven for 10 minutes. Add the venison and marinade to the pan and cook quickly on the Boiling Plate for 4–5 minutes, then add the juniper berries, rosemary, some salt and pepper and sufficient orange juice to cover the meat. Bring to the boil, then cover and cook on the floor of the Simmering Oven for 6 hours.

3 Season the casserole again, then stir in the mushrooms and chestnuts and return the casserole to the Simmering Oven for a further 30 minutes.

4 Prepare the orange garnish. Trim away the ends of the fruit, then cut it into six slices. Heat a little fragrant olive oil or sunflower oil in a frying pan on the Boiling Plate and fry the slices quickly on both sides until lightly browned. Serve the venison with a slice of the fried orange on the side and a small sprig of fresh rosemary.

Mediterranean Roast Leg of Lamb
WITH VEGETABLE GRATIN

Slow Aga-roasted lamb is packed with flavour, especially when crusted with a richly savoury and pungent mix of mustard and olive pâté. The vegetable gratin is all that it is needed on the side.

1 Make small slits all over the lamb with a sharp knife, then squeeze pieces of garlic, rosemary and olives into each slit. Season the meat well on both sides with salt and pepper then mix together the mustard and olive paste and smear generously over the lamb in the roasting tin.

2 Roast in the Roasting Oven for 30 minutes, then transfer to the top of the Simmering Oven for at least 2 hours. Return the lamb to the Roasting Oven for a final 30 minutes to crisp the fat, then leave to stand for 20–30 minutes before carving.

3 Blanch the prepared vegetables for 4–5 minutes in boiling, salted water on top of the Aga – you may need to do this in two batches – then drain. Turn into a buttered gratin dish and mix with the cream, salt, pepper and freshly grated nutmeg.

4 Cook the vegetables for about 40 minutes on the wire shelf at the top of the Roasting Oven while the lamb is resting. Stir the vegetables once during cooking.

5 Overlap slices of lamb on a bed of the vegetables with a garnish of watercress or rocket on top. Spoon some of the creamy vegetable juices over and serve immediately.

Serves 6

1.8kg leg of lamb,
  well trimmed, but not
  completely devoid of fat
1 large clove garlic,
  cut into slivers
1 sprig rosemary
10–12 pitted green olives,
  sliced
coarse sea salt and freshly
  ground black pepper
2 tsp Dijon mustard
2 tsp black olive paste
watercress or rocket,
  to garnish

Vegetable gratin:

1.75kg mixed vegetables,
  such as carrots, potatoes,
  leeks, onions, courgettes,
  coarsely shredded in a
  food processor
300ml/1¼ cups double cream
salt and freshly ground
  black pepper
freshly grated nutmeg

Aga equipment:

large roasting tin on third set
  of runners in Roasting
  Oven, then first set of
  runners in Simmering Oven
wire shelf on second set of
  runners in Roasting Oven

OLIVES

Why is it that an olive so seldom tastes of anything that even vaguely resembles the fleshy, fragrant fruit of the Mediterranean the minute you leave its azure-blue, sun-drenched shores? I am certain it is because the olives have often travelled in brine which, although it is an essential part of the pickling process, does affect their flavour if they steep in it for too long.

Red or black olives are merely green fruits which have been left on the tree to ripen fully. All olives have to be salted or brined before they are ready and it is impossible to eat them straight from the tree.

If you buy your olives in brine (most canned olives are packed in the salty liquor), rinse them thoroughly before use. I always try to crush mine lightly, and then toss them in garlic, herbs and seasonings before steeping them in good olive oil for 30 minutes or so before using them.

VINEGARS

Vinegar is really a by-product of the local brewing industry, thus UK vinegar was usually malt from beer, whilst the French made wine vinegars and the Spanish sherry vinegars. Wine and sherry varieties are generally much less acidic and powerful than malt vinegar, which I really only use for pickling. Certainly wine or sherry vinegars should be used for salad dressings and marinades.

Balsamic vinegar is made in Modena in northern Italy. It is distilled grape must and is very sweet for a vinegar, especially if it has been aged in oak. Balsamic vinegar can become a very valuable commodity, almost an heirloom Closer to home, wine vinegars flavoured with raspberries or strawberries may be used for fruit sauces and stronger flavoured vinegars, for for example made with blackcurrants, make excellent additions to marinades for venison, pheasant and other types of game.

Braised Pheasant
WITH PRUNES, LENTILS & PICKLED WALNUTS

Although Nick and I do not shoot ourselves (or anyone else, for that matter!), we have plenty of friends who do, and are therefore the grateful recipients of plenty of pheasants in the season. Supermarkets now stock the birds – although at rather more than end-of-shoot prices – so you can all try this satisfying winter casserole.

1 Dust the pheasant pieces with the seasoned flour, then brown them quickly all over in the hot oil in an oven-to-hob casserole on top of the Aga. Remove the pheasant with a perforated spoon, then add the prepared vegetables to the pan and cook, covered, on the floor of the Roasting Oven for 10 minutes.

2 Add the wine or sherry and cook on the Boiling Plate until reduced by about half, stirring and scraping up any sediment from the bottom of the pan. Return the browned pheasant to the casserole, then add sufficient stock to cover. Stir in the prunes, lentils, rosemary, bay leaves and seasonings, then bring to the boil. Transfer to the floor of the Simmering Oven for 1½–2 hours, until the pheasant and lentils are just tender.

3 Season the casserole to taste after adding the pickled walnuts. You could serve this casserole with some herb dumplings – check out the recipe for Pork Goulash (page 77) for the method.

Serves 4

2 pheasants, cut into breasts and leg joints (use the remaining carcasses for stock)
1 tbsp seasoned flour
1 tbsp olive oil
1 large onion, finely chopped
1 large carrot, sliced
4 stalks celery, chopped
100ml/½ cup dry white wine or dry sherry
450ml/2 cups stock
8–10 pitted prunes – Pruneaux d'Agen are my favourite
75g/⅓ cup green lentils
1 tbsp freshly chopped rosemary or 2 tsp dried
2 bay leaves
salt and freshly ground black pepper
8–10 pickled walnuts, thickly sliced

Smoked Pheasant Breasts
WITH SPINACH RISOTTO

I am very fond of lightly smoked meats and fish, and have enjoyed exploring smoking in the Aga. The only special equipment you need is fine wood chips – use smoker chips, very fine barbecue chips, or even hardwood shavings if you are into DIY.

Serves 4

4 pheasant breasts, on or off the bone
4 rashers streaky or fatty back bacon

Risotto:

1 red onion, finely sliced
2 tbsp olive oil
250g/1½ cups risotto rice
1.2 litres/5 cups hot vegetable stock
125g fresh spinach, finely shredded
salt and freshly ground black pepper
shavings of Parmesan cheese, to garnish

Aga equipment:

small roasting tin with low rack

1 Heat the tin on the floor of the Roasting Oven for 10–15 minutes. Lightly oil the rack and place the pheasant breasts on it, wrapping each one in a rasher of bacon. Transfer the tin to the Boiling Plate and add the wood chips – they should start to smoke almost immediately. Add the pheasant on the wire rack, then carefully cover the tin with foil – *use your Aga gauntlets as the tin will be very hot*. Leave the tin on the Boiling Plate for 10 minutes to smoke the pheasant.

2 Cook the onion and oil for the risotto for 5 minutes in a covered pan on the floor of the Roasting Oven – choose a pan that will fit into the oven with the roasting tin. Stir the rice into the pan until the grains are well coated with the hot oil, then add the hot stock. Cook, covered, on the floor of the Roasting Oven for 20–25 minutes, adding the shredded spinach and seasoning after 15 minutes and giving the rice a stir. When ready the stock will have been absorbed, leaving a creamy, moist risotto.

3 Transfer the roasting tin to the floor of the Roasting Oven for 10–15 minutes, until the pheasant is just cooked. Serve the breasts, sliced at an angle, on a bed of the risotto, sprinkled with Parmesan shavings.

Spiced Pork, Apricot & Walnut Pie

Hot water crust is probably the easiest pastry to make, and it is very forgiving as you manhandle it into shape! This pie is to be eaten cold, in large wedges, with salad and home-made pickle or pickled walnuts. Once the pie is cut, cover the surface of the filling with plastic wrap for storage but leave the pastry open, which will keep it crisp.

1 To make the pastry, place the flour and salt in a large bowl and make a well in the centre. Melt the lard into the milk and water on top of the Aga, bring to the boil then pour immediately into the flour. Mix to a soft, manageable dough, then turn on to the work surface and knead lightly until smooth. Cover the pastry with the upturned mixing bowl until required.

2 Mix the diced pork with all the remaining ingredients, except the egg and gelatine.

3 Roll out two-thirds of the pastry into a large circle and use it to line the base and sides of a 22.5cm spring-form, loose-bottomed tin. Press the pastry well into the corners and up the sides of the tin. Pack in the filling, pressing it down firmly with the back of a spoon, then roll out the remaining pastry into a circular lid for the pie. Brush the edges of the pastry with egg, then press both crusts together and seal. Use your fingers to press the pastry into a decorative edge. Make a small slit in the centre of the lid to allow the steam to escape.

4 Brush the lid of the pie with egg, then bake on the floor of the Roasting Oven for 1½ hours, inserting the cold shelf after 1 hour, or move the pie to the floor of the Baking Oven in a four-oven Aga at that time. Add a little salt to the remaining beaten egg.

5 Loosen the pie from the edge of the tin before opening, especially if any meat juices have escaped to make the pastry stick. Carefully open the spring, then remove the sides. Place the pie on a baking sheet and brush the sides and top with the salted egg wash. Bake for a further 30–40 minutes, brushing the pie with egg once more during cooking.

Serves 12

1kg boned spare rib of pork, cut into 1cm dice
100g/½ cup ready-to-eat dried apricots, chopped
5cm piece fresh ginger root, coarsely grated and squeezed
1 tbsp green cardamom pods, crushed and seeded
⅛ freshly grated nutmeg
1 orange, grated zest and juice
1 tsp salt
½ tsp freshly ground black pepper
100g/1 cup walnut pieces, roughly chopped
2 tbsp parsley, freshly chopped or chives, freshly snipped
1 large egg, beaten
1 tbsp gelatine or aspic powder

Hot water crust pastry:

450g/3 cups plain flour
2 tsp salt
125g lard
150ml/⅔ cup milk and water, mixed

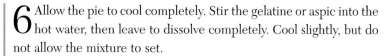

6 Allow the pie to cool completely. Stir the gelatine or aspic into the hot water, then leave to dissolve completely. Cool slightly, but do not allow the mixture to set.

7 Carefully pour the jelly mixture into the pie, until you can force no more in through the slit in the lid. Chill the pie in the fridge for at least 3 hours before slicing and serving.

Mustard & Ginger Crusted Gammon

I quite often cook a small piece of gammon if we are having a quiet weekend on our own – it provides a good meal for us, and there is usually enough left over for sandwiches or a quick Monday meal, like Gammon & Cracked Wheat Risotto (page 47).

Serves 4

1 small joint of gammon, weighing about 1kg, soaked if necessary
5cm piece fresh ginger root
3 tbsp Honeycup or Dijon mustard
4 tbsp fresh white breadcrumbs
salt and freshly ground black pepper
cloves

Aga equipment:
small roasting tin on second or third set of runners in Roasting Oven, depending on the shape of the joint

1 Place the gammon in a suitable pan on an up-turned metal lid or old heatproof saucer – this stops the bottom of the joint from drying out. Cover with fresh cold water and bring to the boil on top of the Aga. Cover the pan and cook on the floor of the Roasting Oven for 30 minutes, then transfer to the floor of the Simmering Oven for a further 1½ hours.

2 Coarsely grate the ginger, then squeeze the juice from it. Beat the juice into the mustard until well blended – you might like to add 1–2 tablespoons of demerara sugar if you are using Dijon mustard, to sweeten the crust. Stir in the breadcrumbs and season lightly.

3 Remove the gammon from the pan and pull or trim away the skin. Score the fat and place the joint in the small roasting tin. Press the crust into the fat and stud it with a few cloves. Cook for 10 minutes in the Roasting Oven until evenly browned. Stand the joint for 10–15 minutes before carving.

Roast Goose

WITH PRUNE-STUFFED APPLES

It's very easy to say that we should make more use of goose but, for most of us, it's an expensive treat reserved for Christmas and other celebrations. Its limited season begins at Michaelmas on 29 September and finishes just a few short weeks later at the end of December. If you do treat yourself to a goose, the Aga is, of course, the ultimate stress-free way of cooking it to perfection. Geese may live for up to forty years but they are never sold for the pot older than eighteen months. A Christmas goose may be almost twice as heavy as a young bird sold at Michaelmas.

1 Pull any excess fat from the neck of the goose – *goose fat is the best for roasting potatoes* – then prick the bird all over with a fork and place breast side down, on the rack in the roasting tin. Cook for 45 minutes in the Roasting Oven until the bird is lightly browned all over, turning it after 30 minutes.

2 Transfer the goose to the Simmering Oven and cook for a further 2 hours, until a skewer inserted through the thickest part of the goose, the thigh, releases only clear juices. *You may wish to drain off and reserve some of the fat during cooking.*

3 Prepare the stuffing for the apples. Cook the onion and celery in the butter in a small covered pan for 5 minutes on the floor of the Roasting Oven, then add all the other stuffing ingredients with some salt and pepper. Cut the apples in half horizontally, then cut out the core with a small sharp knife. Pile the stuffing into the cavities then mound it up over the apples.

4 Return the goose to the Roasting Oven for 20 minutes to crisp the skin, then leave it to stand for 15–20 minutes before carving. Place the apples in a small tin and roast on the wire shelf in the Roasting Oven for 10–12 minutes, while the goose is resting. Serve one stuffed apple with each helping of thinly carved meat.

Serves 6

1 goose, weighing about
   4.5–5kg
salt and freshly ground
   black pepper

Prune stuffing:

1 onion, finely chopped
3 stalks celery, finely
   chopped
25g butter
125g pitted ready-to-eat
   prunes
50g walnut pieces or
   chopped chestnuts
150g fresh wholewheat
   breadcrumbs
salt and freshly ground
   black pepper
3 Cox's Orange Pippin eating
   apples

Aga equipment:

large roasting tin with low
   rack on fourth set of
   runners in Roasting Oven,
   then third set of runners in
   Simmering Oven
wire shelf on third set of
   runners in Roasting Oven

Normandy Pork Goes South

Normandy Pheasant, Normandy Chicken – such a description usually means cooked with the classic combination of apples, cream and calvados. Let's move it all towards the Med, and add some tapenade for a little piquancy.

Serves 4

1 thick pork fillet or tenderloin, weighing about 500g
2 tbsp olive oil
knob of butter
salt and freshly ground black pepper
1 tbsp tapenade or black olive paste
1 tart green eating apple, such as Granny Smith
1 small onion, finely chopped
1 small clove garlic, crushed
150ml/⅔ cup dry cider
1–2 tbsp calvados (optional)
150ml/⅔ cup double cream

Aga equipment:

small roasting tin on second set of runners in Roasting Oven

1 Brown the pork in the oil and butter in a large frying pan on top of the Aga. Season the fillet lightly, then smear it with tapenade and transfer it to the roasting tin. Roast for 30–40 minutes, then allow it to stand and rest for 10–15 minutes.

2 Core the apple, cut away and discard the top and bottom then cut the fruit into 4 thick slices. Fry them until lightly golden in the pan juices from browning the pork, then keep the apple warm on a plate in the Simmering Oven.

3 Add the onion to the frying pan and cook on the Simmering Plate until just soft. Stir in the cider, then boil quickly until reduced by half. Add the calvados, if using, and the cream. Boil until slightly thickened and lightly browned. Season the sauce to taste.

4 Slice the pork fillet obliquely, then serve the slices garnished with the fried apple, and with the sauce spooned round.

Desserts

Pear & Chocolate Charlottes

These delicious puds are a bit of a fiddle to prepare, but are well worth the effort. When I am ultra-organised and enormously fond of the people coming to dinner I bake my own brioche to line the moulds, but a bought brioche, or regular white bread also produces delicious results. Serve the puddings in a pool of vanilla custard, and with a goodly dollop of lightly whipped cream. Try the same puds with chopped apple and few blueberries, but add some sugar to the filling.

1 Generously butter six individual pudding moulds, then coat the insides with demerara sugar, tipping it from one mould to the next. Cut six circles of bread to fit the base of the moulds, then cut the remaining slices into pieces to line the sides. Dip each piece in melted butter, then squeeze them into the moulds, leaving no gaps at all for the filling to show through.

2 Cook the pears with the water and lemon juice in a covered pan on the floor of the Roasting Oven for 5 minutes, or until just tender, then leave covered until cold. The length of cooking time will depend on the ripeness of the pears.

3 Scoop the pieces of pear from the liquor using a perforated spoon, and pack them into the bread-lined tins, mixing the chocolate chips into the fruit. Cut circles of bread to fit the tops of the tins over the fruit, dipping them in the remaining melted butter. *The charlottes can easily be prepared in advance to this stage if you are entertaining.*

4 Place the charlottes on a baking sheet, then cook in the Roasting Oven for 30 minutes. Slip a sharp knife in around the sides of the moulds to loosen the puddings, then invert them on to warmed serving plates.

Serves 6

150g unsalted butter, melted
150g/1 cup demerara sugar (approximately)
8 slices from a large loaf, crusts removed
3–4 large firm dessert pears, peeled, cored and cut into large dice
1–2 tbsp water
lemon juice
40g good quality chocolate chips (I cut my own from my favourite bitter chocolate)

Aga equipment:

wire shelf on third set of runners in Roasting Oven

Crème Caramel

My version of this all-time favourite is lightly spiced and rather deliciously different. Ignore the spicing and you have the classic dessert. I often wonder why any other puddings have been created!

Serves 6

butter for greasing
3 large eggs
50g/⅓ cup caster sugar
500ml/2½ cups whipping cream
1 vanilla pod
2 large cinnamon sticks, broken
1 tsp green cardamom pods, crushed

Caramel:

175g/1 cup caster sugar

Aga equipment:

small roasting tin on fourth set of runners in Roasting Oven

1 Lightly butter a 1 litre soufflé dish. Heat the sugar for the caramel, preferably in a non-stick pan, on the Simmering Plate until melted, shaking it in the pan occasionally until dissolved. Bring quickly to the boil and cook until lightly golden, then pour into the prepared dish. Tip the dish this way and that, until the caramel completely coats the base and sides.

2 Whisk the eggs and sugar together until pale. Heat the cream in the caramel pan with the vanilla pod and cinnamon sticks until almost boiling, then pour it on to the eggs, stirring all the time. Have a kettle on the side of the Boiling Plate, heating up throughout this stage.

3 Strain the custard over the caramel in the soufflé dish, then cover the dish with foil to prevent a crust forming during baking. Place the dish in the roasting tin, then pour boiling water around it to half fill the tin. Cook in the Roasting Oven for 20 minutes, then transfer the tin to the floor of the Simmering Oven for a further hour.

4 Leave to cool completely, then chill the crème caramel for as long as possible, preferably overnight, in the fridge.

5 Loosen round the edges of the cream with a sharp knife, then invert the caramel on a deep serving dish, leaving the dish in place. Put in the fridge for about an hour before serving, then remove the dish. All the caramel will be caught, ready for you to spoon over each helping.

Rhubarb & Angelica Tart

I love rhubarb, the herald of spring, especially when cooked with a few angelica leaves, which takes away some of the tartness of the fruit. The rhubarb is lightly poached and then covered with brown sugar, which could be quickly caramelised with a blow torch if you have one.

1 Rub the butter into the flour for the pastry. Stir in the sugar then mix the crumbs to a firm dough with cold water. Roll out the pastry on a lightly floured surface and use it to line a shallow 22.5–25cm loose-bottomed flan tin. Chill the pastry for at least 20 minutes.

2 Prick the base of the pastry all over with a fork, then line with greaseproof paper and baking beans. Cook on the floor of the Roasting Oven for 15 minutes, then carefully remove the paper and beans and cook for a further 5 minutes, until the base has dried out.

3 Blend the eggs yolks with the sugar and cornflour to make a smooth paste. Heat the cream on the Simmering Plate until almost boiling, then pour it on to the eggs, stirring all the time. Rinse the pan out with cold water, then return the custard to it and heat on the Simmering Plate, stirring all the time, until the mixture has thickened but not boiled. Pour the custard into the pastry case and allow it to cool while preparing the rhubarb.

4 Poach the rhubarb with the angelica leaf in a pan of just simmering water on the Simmering Plate for 8–10 minutes – the rhubarb pieces should retain their shape.

5 Remove the rhubarb pieces from the water with a perforated spoon and arrange them over the custard, then scatter them with the demerara sugar just before serving.

Serves 6–8

3 large egg yolks
50g/⅓ cup caster sugar
1 tsp cornflour
300ml/1¼ cups single cream
450g rhubarb, trimmed and
   cut into 5cm lengths
1 angelica leaf, roughly torn
3 tbsp demerara sugar

Pastry:

75g butter
150g/1 cup plain flour
1 tbsp sugar
cold water

Apricot Pecan Pie

I'm not sure that I have ever had a real pecan pie because I like to mix the sweet nuts with some dried fruits, for extra flavour. You could try this with figs, but the apricots add a sweet sharpness to the mix.

Serves 8–10
100g butter
175g/1⅛ cup plain flour
pinch of salt
1 tsp caster sugar
1 large egg yolk
cold water

Filling:
125g unsalted butter
100g/⅔ cup caster sugar
4 tbsp/⅓ cup clear honey
½ tsp ground mace
100ml/½ cup orange juice
200g/1 cup ready-to-eat dried apricots, finely chopped
200g/2 cups pecan nuts, half chopped and the remainder left whole
extra honey for brushing

Aga equipment:
cold shelf on second set of runners in Roasting Oven

1 Rub the butter into the flour, salt and sugar, until the mixture resembles fine breadcrumbs. Mix to a manageable dough with the egg yolk and any cold water that is necessary. Roll out the pastry on a lightly floured surface and use it to line a 25cm/10 inch loose-bottomed flan tin. Flute the rim of the pastry between your fingertips, then chill it for about 30 minutes, while preparing the filling.

2 Cream together the butter and sugar until pale and fluffy, then beat in the honey. Add the mace and orange juice and continue mixing until blended. The mixture may appear curdled, but do not worry.

3 Add the apricots and the chopped pecans and mix well, then turn the mixture into the chilled pastry case and spread it evenly. Arrange the whole pecan halves over the filling and brush them with a little extra honey if you have the inclination. Bake on the Roasting Oven floor with the cold shelf in position for 30 minutes, or on the floor of the four-oven Aga Baking Oven for 45 minutes. Allow the tart to cool slightly before serving.

Almond Roulade
WITH LEMON GRASS ICE-CREAM

I became hooked on ice-cream when I wrote a book about ice-cream machines. Make your own, and a whole world of flavours is available to you. Lemon grass, a surprisingly sophisticated flavour, is one of my favourites. If you don't have an ice-cream machine, you can freeze the ice in the freezer. I do not find it necessary to keep beating during freezing if the mixture is well chilled before freezing. Fill the roulade while the ice-cream is still slightly soft, or allow it to soften slightly if previously frozen.

1 Slowly heat the single cream on the Simmering Plate with the lemon grass, cardamom seeds and lime zest until almost boiling, then cover and leave to infuse for 20 minutes. Strain into a clean pan.

2 Whisk the egg yolks and sugar until pale and thick – it is best to do this by hand as you don't want the mixture full of air bubbles. Reheat the cream until almost boiling, then pour it on to the eggs, whisking all the time. Add the lime juice. Rinse the pan in cold water, then return the custard to it and cook slowly on the Simmering Plate, stirring all the time, for 2–3 minutes, until slightly thickened – just enough to coat the back of the wooden spoon. *Do not overcook the custard or the eggs will curdle.* Turn into a clean bowl and leave until completely cold, then chill well.

3 Prepare the roulade. Line a Swiss roll tin, about 20x27.5cm, with baking parchment. Whisk the eggs and sugar until pale and thick, then fold in the almonds and baking powder – *I always find this easiest using a wire balloon whisk.* Spread the mixture evenly in the tin – don't push out all the air – then bake in the Roasting Oven, with the cold shelf in position, for about 15 minutes until just set.

4 Lay a piece of baking parchment on a wire rack and scatter it with caster sugar. Invert the cooked roulade on to the rack and remove the lining paper. Trim away the edges and leave until cold.

5 Whisk the whipping cream until thick and floppy then fold it into the lemon grass cream. Scoop into an ice-cream maker and freeze

Serves 4–6

300ml/1¼ cups single cream
2 fresh stalks lemon grass, bruised and chopped
seeds from 12 green cardamom pods, crushed
1 lime, grated zest and juice
4 large egg yolks
75g/½ cup caster sugar
300ml/1¼ cups whipping cream

Roulade:

4 large eggs
125g/⅔ cup caster sugar
75g/1 generous cup ground almonds
1 tsp baking powder

Aga equipment:

wire shelf on fourth set of runners in Roasting Oven, with cold shelf on first set of runners churn until ready to serve. Scoop the ice-cream into the centre of the sponge, then roll it up so that the ice-cream is completely enclosed in the sponge, using the paper to help you. Harden in the freezer for at least 30 minutes.

6 You may need to soften the roulade in the fridge for about 30 minutes before serving if you allow it to freeze completely.

Luscious Lemon Tart

There is no other way to describe this, a rich, lemony egg custard tart in a rich almond pastry crust. A blackberry or raspberry coulis makes a wonderful drizzle with the tart.

Serves 6–8

100g unsalted butter
150g/1 cup plain flour
1 tbsp caster sugar
50g/⅔ cup ground almonds
1 large egg, beaten
sifted icing sugar for dredging

Filling:

4 large eggs
200g/1⅓ cups caster sugar
4 lemons, grated zest and juice
300ml/1¼ cups whipping cream

Aga equipment:

cold shelf on third set of runners in Roasting Oven

1 Rub the butter into the flour and sugar, then stir in the almonds and bind the pastry together with the beaten egg. Roll the pastry out on a lightly floured surface and use it to line a deep 20cm flan tin with a removable base. Crimp the edges, then chill the pastry for about an hour – it needs a longer chilling because of the almonds in the crust, which may be inclined to oil after kneading.

2 Line the pastry case with greaseproof paper and fill with baking beans. Bake on the floor of the Roasting Oven with the cold shelf in for 15 minutes.

3 Prepare the filling while the pastry is cooking. Whisk the eggs and sugar together until pale, then add the lemon zest and juice. Fold in the cream then pour the mixture into the pastry case. Return to the Roasting Oven for 10 minutes, after which time the filling will have a lightly golden crust. Carefully transfer the tart to the floor of the Simmering Oven and cook for 45–60 minutes, until just set, or for 30–40 minutes on the floor of the four-oven Aga Baking Oven.

4 Allow the tart to cool completely, then dredge it with sifted icing sugar before serving.

Hugh's Pudding

Pavlova is an Australian dessert created in Perth by chef Sachse of The Esplanade Hotel in the early 1930s. I made a huge one for a supper party to send our friends Anna and Hugh off on an adventure which took them from Perth to Brisbane. Waxing lyrical about the chewy but crisp texture of the Aga meringue (exactly the texture that Sachse was trying to create), Hugh declared this pudding his favourite – so now it's called Hugh's pudding.

1 Mark a 25cm circle on a large sheet of baking parchment laid on a baking sheet. Sprinkle the circle lightly with caster sugar – this makes it easier to remove the cooked pavlova.

2 Whisk the egg whites with a pinch of salt until they are really stiff – start off gradually then increase speed for maximum bulk. The age old trick to see when the egg whites are ready is to tip the bowl upside down over your head. They should stay in the bowl...

3 Mix the sugar with the cream of tartar and cornflour and gradually whisk half into the egg whites. Whisk in the vanilla and vinegar, then the remaining sugar. Scrape the meringue from the bowl and spread it lightly over the prepared baking sheet, using the circle to achieve a round pavlova. Pull the meringue up into a decorative edge and make the centre slightly thinner than the edges. Bake in the Simmering Oven for 3–4 hours, until the pavlova is dry, lightly browned and slightly cracked. Cool on the paper on a wire rack.

4 Cut the skin from the pineapple and remove the core. Whizz the flesh for just a few seconds to give a fresh pineapple crush. *Drain away the juices and enjoy drinking them – a perfect excuse for a pina colada!* Whip the cream until thick and floppy then fold in the pineapple and mint – add a little sugar if necessary. Pile the cream over the meringue on a large serving plate.

5 Melt the chocolate in a small bowl over a pan of water on the Simmering Plate. Scoop the melted chocolate into a paper forcing bag, then drizzle it in sweeping lines across the pavlova, forwards and back, to make a kind of lattice. Decorate with fresh mint leaves just before serving.

Serves 8

caster sugar for sprinkling
4 large egg whites
pinch of salt
225g/1½ cups caster sugar
½ tsp cream of tartar
1 level tbsp cornflour
½ tsp natural vanilla extract
1 tsp white wine vinegar
  (optional – I never seem to
  have any, but the meringue
  always works!)
1 small fresh pineapple
300ml/1¼ cups whipping
  cream
1–2 tsp freshly chopped mint
50g bitter chocolate
fresh mint leaves, to decorate

Aga equipment:

wire shelf on third set of
  runners in Simmering Oven

Prune & Walnut Egg Custard Tart

I don't know why prunes are so mocked – soft and juicy, they are one of the most delicious fruits there are. The mixture of prunes and walnuts is very French. Home-made nutmeg-flavoured ice-cream or just plain cream is the perfect accompaniment.

Serves 6–8

100g butter
175g/1⅓ cups plain flour
1 tsp caster sugar
cold water
125g/⅔ cup ready-to-eat pitted prunes, roughly chopped
50g/⅓ cup walnut pieces, roughly chopped
2 large eggs, beaten
1 tbsp caster sugar
300ml/1¼ cups single cream
freshly grated nutmeg

Aga equipment:

cold shelf on fourth set of runners in Roasting Oven

1 Rub the butter into the flour and sugar until the mixture resembles fine breadcrumbs, then bind it together with just enough cold water to give a firm, manageable dough. Knead lightly on a floured surface and shape the pastry into a smooth ball, then roll it out and use to line a deep 20cm flan tin or sandwich tin with a removable base. Crimp the edges of the pastry between your fingers, then chill the pastry case for 20 minutes.

2 Scatter the prunes and walnuts evenly over the base of the pastry. Beat the eggs and sugar into the cream, then strain this mixture into the pastry case, and grate some nutmeg over the surface.

3 Bake the tart on the floor of the Roasting Oven with the cold shelf in position for 30 minutes, or until just set, or transfer to the floor of the Baking Oven after 10 minutes and cook for a further 30–40 minutes. Cool slightly, then serve warm or at room temperature, with cream or ice-cream.

Rhubarb & Raspberry Fool

Don't worry – I haven't got my seasons confused! I use frozen raspberries with young spring rhubarb to bring a touch of luxury to this simple dessert. The fruit mixture also makes a deliciously different topping for a spring pavlova.

1 Place the rhubarb, frozen raspberries, wine, sugar and star anise in a covered pan and cook on the floor of the Roasting Oven for 20 minutes, until the rhubarb is soft. Taste the fruit and add any extra sugar that is necessary, then leave it to cool completely.

2 Remove the star anise, then whizz the fruits with all the juice until smooth. Whip the cream until thick but not hard, then fold in the fruit purée. Spoon into a large serving dish or individual glasses and chill. Decorate with long strips of angelica and serve with short-bread biscuits.

Serves 6–8

500g young rhubarb, trimmed and cut into 2.5cm chunks
250g frozen raspberries
150ml/⅔ cup sweet dessert wine
75g/½ cup soft brown sugar
2 pieces of star anise
450ml/2 cups whipping or double cream
angelica strips, to decorate
shortbread biscuits, to serve

Janie Suthering's Treacle Tart

As my friend Janie says, what sort of a treacle tart is it if you just mix syrup and breadcrumbs together for the filling? Be warned – this is utterly addictive!

1 Rub the butter into the flour and salt until the mixture resembles fine breadcrumbs, then add sufficient cold water to mix to a firm dough. Roll out the pastry on a lightly floured work surface and use to line a 22.5–25cm loose-bottomed flan tin. Crimp the edges of the pastry to give a decorative crust.

2 Mix all the ingredients for the filling together, then spoon them into the pastry case. Bake the treacle tart on the floor of the

Serves 8–10

125g butter
225g/1¾ cups plain flour
pinch of salt
cold water

Filling:

350g/1½ cups golden syrup
50g/⅔ cup ground almonds

grated zest and juice of half
a lemon
150ml/⅔ cup double cream
75g/1 cup fresh white
breadcrumbs
1 large egg, beaten

Aga equipment:

cold shelf on third set of
runners in Roasting Oven

Roasting Oven for 30 minutes, inserting the cold shelf after 20 minutes to prevent the filling from becoming too brown or bake for 10 minutes in the Roasting Oven and a further 30 minutes on the floor of the four-oven Aga Baking Oven.

3 Cool slightly before serving in not-too-generous slices, with whatever accompaniment your conscience will allow although it is quite delicious served just as it is.

Baked Figs

WITH ALMONDS & HONEYED MASCARPONE

I fantasise about using fresh figs, straight from the garden, but common sense tells me I would just eat such treasures fresh from the tree. So, ready-to-eat dried figs are gently baked and then topped with the easiest of luxury toppings.

Serves 6–8

500g ready-to-eat dried figs,
roughly chopped
50g blanched almonds – or
use Brazil nuts if you prefer
2 oranges, grated zest
and juice
250g mascarpone cheese
50ml milk
2 tbsp honey

Aga equipment:

wire shelf on fourth set of
runners in Roasting Oven,
with cold shelf on second
set of runners
OR wire shelf on third set of
runners in four-oven Aga
Baking Oven

1 Place the figs and almonds in a small ovenproof dish, then add the orange zest and juice. Cover the dish, use foil if it does not have a suitable lid, and cook in the Roasting Oven for 20 minutes, or for 30 minutes in the four-oven Aga Baking Oven.

2 Beat the mascarpone with a little milk if it is very thick, then add honey to taste. I sometimes use a set clover or orange blossom honey, or a runny acacia honey. If your honey is very hard, warm it on the back of the Aga until soft, or place the jar in a pan of hot water.

3 Serve the figs warm, with a huge dollop of the mascarpone cream as an accompaniment.

Baked Pears

WITH LEMON GRASS & PISTACHIO SYRUP

Inspired by Phil Vickery, the chef at The Castle Hotel in Taunton and, I think, one of the hottest talents today in British cookery, this is a welcome change from the more predictable pears in red wine. Phil serves his pears with a shortbread biscuit and sharp blackcurrant coulis – I take an easier option and revel in them just as they are in this somewhat adapted recipe. The syrup is spooned over the pears to moisten them just before serving – some rich vanilla ice-cream would complete the dish perfectly.

1 Place the vanilla pod in a small covered pan with the sugar, water, lemon zest and lemon grass. Cook on the floor of the Roasting Oven for 10 minutes, stirring once. Leave the syrup to infuse for 20–30 minutes.

2 Place the pears in a small buttered ovenproof dish, pour the juice of half the lemon over them and dot with the butter. Bake the pears on the floor of the Roasting Oven for 15 minutes, spooning the buttery juices over them once or twice during cooking. Add the pistachio nuts, then leave the pears to cool slightly.

3 Strain the syrup to remove the flavourings, then spoon it over the pears to serve.

Serves 4

1 vanilla pod
75g/½ cup caster sugar
250ml/1 cup water
1 lemon, pared zest and juice
1 large stalk lemon grass, bruised
4 large ripe but firm pears, peeled, cored and sliced
25g unsalted butter, cut into slivers
25g/⅓ cup pistachio nuts

The Ultimate Chocolate Pudding

I am sure that every one of us has our own idea or dream of the ultimate chocolate pudding – well, this is mine. It's like a baked chocolate mousse cake and utterly delicious although, as with all chocolate recipes, much depends on your choice of chocolate. Use the best you possibly can, and preferably one with 70 per cent cocoa solids.

Serves 8–10

200g fine plain chocolate, broken into small pieces
200g unsalted butter
4 large eggs, separated
200g/1½cups caster sugar
icing sugar for dredging
crème fraîche, thick Greek yogurt, ice-cream or fresh berries, to serve

Aga equipment:

wire shelf on fourth set of runners in Roasting Oven with cold shelf on first set of runners

1 Line a 22.5cm loose-bottomed tin with baking parchment – a spring-form tin is best if you have one. Melt the chocolate in a large bowl over a pan of hot water on the Simmering Plate, then add the butter and stir until it has melted, blending into the chocolate. Allow to cool slightly.

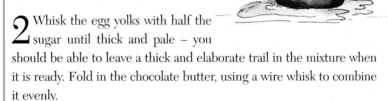

2 Whisk the egg yolks with half the sugar until thick and pale – you should be able to leave a thick and elaborate trail in the mixture when it is ready. Fold in the chocolate butter, using a wire whisk to combine it evenly.

3 Whisk the egg whites until stiff, then gradually whisk in the remaining sugar to give a glossy meringue. Fold the egg whites into the chocolate mixture, then scrape the mixture into the prepared tin.

4 Bake in the Roasting oven with the cold shelf for 40 minutes, until just set, or for about an hour in the four-oven Aga Baking Oven, with the wire shelf on the third set of runners. Leave to cool slightly. *The cake may sink a little, but don't worry.*

5 Carefully release the cake from the tin – run a thin-bladed knife around the mixture before peeling away the baking parchment.

6 Dredge with icing sugar. Serve either warm or completely cold with crème fraîche, Greek yogurt, ice-cream or fresh berries.

Rice Pudding

We have eaten more rice puddings since we had the Aga than you would believe possible! How can such a simple dish be so delicious? The creamier the milk that you use, the creamier the pudding. Try using coconut milk with a hint of spice for something a little bit different.

1 Butter a 750ml ovenproof dish, then place the rice and sugar in the bottom. Pour in the milk, give a quick stir then dot the top of the milk with slivers of butter and cover it with freshly grated nutmeg.

2 Bake the pudding in the Roasting Oven for 20 minutes, until a light golden skin has formed. Transfer the pudding to the Simmering Oven and cook for a further 2 hours. If you like a milky, slightly runny pudding cook on the shelf in the Simmering Oven – for a more solid result, bake directly on the floor of the oven.

3 Serve the rice pudding with a good spoonful of the jam of your choice.

Should serve 4!

50g/⅓ cup short-grain
    pudding rice
1 tbsp caster sugar
500ml/2½ cups milk
knob of butter, cut into slivers
freshly grated nutmeg

Aga equipment:

wire shelf on fourth set of
    runners in Roasting Oven,
then wire shelf on third set of
    runners in Simmering Oven

Bread & Butter Pudding
WITH CROISSANTS

There has been a real revival in the popularity of what must surely be called Nursery Puddings – the favourite desserts of childhood. This is an updated version of a classic, using croissants to give a light and flaky texture to a winter classic. Use good quality chocolate chopped roughly, rather than commercial chocolate chips.

Serves 4

4 large or 6 small croissants
unsalted butter
75g good quality chocolate,
chopped into chips
500ml/2¼ cups milk
3 large eggs, beaten
2 tbsp caster sugar
natural vanilla extract
crème fraîche, to serve

Aga equipment:

wire shelf on fourth set of
runners in Roasting Oven
with cold shelf on first set
of runners

1 Butter a 20cm ovenproof dish. Halve the croissants lengthways and butter them lightly, then scatter the chocolate chips over the butter, pressing them in lightly. Overlap the croissant halves in the buttered dish with the chocolatey buttered sides downwards – this way the custard will stay a better colour during baking and the chocolate will be a surprise for your guests.

2 Whisk the milk with the beaten eggs and sugar and just a few drops of vanilla, then strain the custard into the dish over the croissants. If possible, allow the pudding to stand for half an hour before baking, to allow the croissants to really soak up the custard. Bake the pudding for about 30 minutes – the actual time will depend on your dish and whether you have been able to leave the mixture to stand before baking.

3 Allow to cool slightly before serving warm. A goodly dollop of crème fraîche would be perfect with each helping.

Cakes and Bakes

Cinnamon Apple Cake

A spicy apple cake that could easily be served hot as a pudding with custard, in which case serve the left-overs as cake!

1 Cream together all the ingredients for the cake until the mixture is pale and fluffy – it should be of a very soft dropping consistency.

2 Spread the cake mixture lightly but evenly into the tin which you have prepared.

3 Peel, core and quarter the apples then score them with a fork to give a ridged effect, then press them lightly into the cake. Bake for 25–30 minutes, turning the tin once during baking. *This helps to brown the apples evenly.*

Makes 16–20 pieces

150g soft margarine
150g/1 cup caster sugar
200g/1¾cups self-raising flour
1 heaped tsp baking powder
2 large eggs, beaten
1 tsp cinnamon
few drops vanilla essence
3 tbsp warm water
3 tart green eating apples such as Granny Smith's

Aga equipment:

small roasting tin, lined, on fourth set of runners in Roasting Oven with cold shelf on second set of runners OR second set of runners in Baking Oven of four-oven Aga

All-Butter Almond Shortbread

My mother always makes shortbread in a large round, so that's the way that I do it. I move the shortbread from the Roasting Oven to the Simmering Oven and use the cold shelf for perfect results.

1 Place all the dry ingredients in a bowl and rub in the butter. Continue until the mixture comes together, then press it into a deep 17.5cm sandwich tin. Mark the shortbread into eight with a sharp knife, then decorate the edges with the back of a fork and prick the shortbread all over.

Makes 8 pieces

175g/1¼ cup plain flour
50g/½ cup ground almonds
pinch of salt
65g/⅓ cup caster sugar

150g butter
caster sugar for sprinkling

Aga equipment:

wire shelf on fourth set of runners in Roasting Oven with cold shelf on second set of runners, then cold shelf on second set of runners in Simmering Oven

2 Bake in the Roasting Oven for 20 minutes, until just golden around the edges of the tin. Transfer the now-hot cold shelf (can't think of any other way to describe it!) to the second set of runners in the Simmering Oven and place the shortbread on the shelf. Bake for a further 30 minutes, until golden brown, or bake for 40 minutes on the wire shelf on the third set of runners in the four-oven Aga Baking Oven.

3 Mark the shortbread into portions again, then sprinkle caster sugar over it and leave to cool completely in the tin before cutting into eight.

Rich Dark Chocolate Cake

This is based on a recipe that I learned long ago at College and keep going back to. The black treacle really helps to accentuate the richness of the chocolate.

Makes 16–20 pieces

250g/1⅔ cups self-raising flour
3 tbsp cocoa powder
2 tsp baking powder
pinch of salt
125g/1 cup light soft muscavado sugar
125g butter
150g/½ cup golden syrup
150g/½ cup black treacle
1 large egg, beaten
150ml/⅔ cup milk

Aga equipment:

small roasting tin, lined, on fourth set of runners in Roasting Oven with cold shelf on second set of runners OR second set of runners in Baking Oven of four-oven Aga

1 Sieve the flour, cocoa, baking powder and salt together into a large bowl.

2 Heat all the remaining ingredients in a pan on the Simmering Plate, except the egg and milk, until the butter has just melted. Allow to cool slightly, then beat in the egg and milk.

3 Pour the mixture into the dry ingredients and mix quickly and thoroughly. Spoon into the prepared tin and bake in the Roasting Oven for 25–30 minutes, or for about 40 minutes in the four-oven Aga Baking Oven.

4 When the cake is cooked mark it into squares, then cool on a wire rack.

Chocolate Fudge Fingers

These seem to be everyone's favourite! If you want your shortbread fingers to be the best, do use good chocolate and not a cheap substitute for the topping.

1 Rub the butter into the flour and sugar for the base, until the mixture resembles fine breadcrumbs. Press the crumbs into an even layer over the base of the lined tin and smooth with a palette knife. Bake for 5 minutes in the Roasting Oven, then transfer to the Simmering Oven for a further 20 minutes, until pale golden and set. Leave the shortbread to cool in the tin.

2 Melt the butter for the filling on the floor of the Roasting Oven for 3–4 minutes, then add the condensed milk and golden syrup. Beat thoroughly, to ensure that the ingredients are well blended together, then return the pan to the floor of the oven for a further 10 minutes, stirring once. Move the pan up on to the Simmering Plate and bring the filling to the boil, stirring all the time. Continue cooking for 2–3 minutes, stirring constantly, then pour the thickened fudge mixture over the shortbread in the tin. Leave until cold and set.

3 Heat the chocolate in a bowl over a pan of water on the Boiling Plate, stirring until the chocolate has melted. Do not allow the water to boil – transfer the pan to the Simmering Plate if necessary. Spread the melted chocolate over the fudge filling, mark into squares and leave until cold before cutting.

Makes about 24 pieces

Base:

100g butter
150g/1 cup plain flour
50g/⅓ cup caster sugar

Filling:

250g unsalted butter, cut into small pieces
405g can condensed milk
4 tbsp/⅓ cup golden syrup

Topping:

300g plain chocolate, broken into pieces

Aga equipment:

small roasting tin, lined, on fourth set of runners in Roasting Oven,
then second set of runners in Simmering Oven

Ginger & Marmalade Cake

A quick-mix, quick-bake cake that will quickly disappear!

Makes 16–20 pieces

250g/1⅘ cups self-raising flour
2 tsp baking powder
2 tsp ground ginger
pinch of salt
1 lemon, grated zest
150g/1 cup demerara sugar
125g butter
150g/½ cup golden syrup
150g/½ cup clear honey
2 tbsp marmalade
1 large egg, beaten
150ml/⅔ cup milk

Aga equipment:

small roasting tin, lined, on fourth set of runners in Roasting Oven with cold shelf on second set of runners OR second set of runners in Baking Oven of four-oven Aga

1 Sift the flour, ginger, baking powder and salt together into a large bowl. Heat all the remaining ingredients in a pan on the Simmering Plate, except the egg and milk, until the butter has just melted. Allow to cool slightly, then beat in the egg and milk. Pour the mixture into the dry ingredients and mix quickly and thoroughly.

2 Scrape into the prepared tin and bake in the Roasting Oven for 25–30 minutes, or for 40–45 minutes in the four-oven Aga Baking Oven. Mark into squares, then transfer to a wire rack to cool completely before cutting.

Lemon Poppy Seed Cake

A light, nutty cake with a tang of fresh lemon.

1 Place the poppy seeds in a pan with the grated lemon zest, the juice of one lemon and the milk. Heat on the Simmering Plate for 3–4 minutes, then leave until required. This will slightly soften the seeds – they will still have a nutty taste but the texture will not be quite so firm. *Don't worry if the milk appears to curdle.*

2 Cream together all the remaining ingredients except the egg whites, then add the poppy seed mixture. Whisk the egg whites until stiff then fold them into the mixture and spoon immediately into the prepared tin. Bake for 30 minutes, until set.

3 Blend the extra caster sugar with the juice of the remaining lemon, then drizzle the mixture over the cake as soon as it is cooked. Carefully lift the cake on to a wire cooling rack and leave until cold before cutting into squares.

Makes 16–20 pieces

100g blue poppy seeds
2 lemons, grated zest and
    juice
250ml/1 cup milk
250g soft margarine
250g/1⅛ cups caster sugar
300g/2½ cups self-raising
    flour
2 tsp baking powder
1 tsp bicarbonate of soda
4 large eggs, separated
2 tbsp caster sugar

Aga equipment:

large roasting tin, lined, on
    third set of runners in
    Roasting Oven with cold
    shelf on second set of
    runners OR second set of
    runners in Baking Oven of
    four-oven Aga

Banana & Raisin Muffins

These moist cakes are really quick to make and bake – do not overmix them or they will be heavy.

Makes 12

300g/2 cups fine wholewheat flour
1½ tsp baking powder
½ tsp bicarbonate of soda
1 tsp ground ginger
75g/⅓ cup raisins
75g/½ cup light muscavado sugar
3 large bananas, roughly mashed with a fork
1 tbsp butter, melted and cooled
200ml/1 cup buttermilk
2 large eggs, beaten
sugar for dredging

Aga equipment:

wire shelf on fourth set of runners in Roasting Oven with cold shelf on top set of runners
OR wire shelf on second set of runners in Baking Oven of four-oven Aga

1 Line 12 deep muffin tins with double bun paper cases. Mix together all the dry ingredients, then spoon the bananas into the centre. Add the butter, buttermilk and eggs, then quickly mix the ingredients together with a palette knife until just combined, using quick, deft cutting actions.

2 Quickly divide the muffin mixture between the bun cases, then bake for 20–25 minutes. Scatter a little extra sugar over the muffins as soon as they are cooked and cool on a wire rack.

Wholewheat Hot-Cross Buns

There is nothing like the taste of a home-made hot cross bun! We like ours to be really spicy, and made with a mixture of white and wholewheat flours. I even managed to bribe the neighbours with these buns into putting up our greenhouse!

1 Crumble the yeast into the warm milk and leave to stand for 3–4 minutes. Mix the flours, salt and spices in a large bowl and rub in the butter. Stir in the sugar, then add the yeast liquid and egg. Mix to a manageable dough, adding a little extra milk or water if necessary.

2 Turn the dough out on to a floured surface and knead it thoroughly for up to 10 minutes, until smooth, stretchy and not at all sticky. Flour the bowl lightly, return the dough to it and cover, then leave by the side of the Aga for about 1–1½ hours, until well risen and doubled in size. *This dough is richer than most and therefore takes longer to rise.*

3 Gently re-knead the dough – this is called knocking back – whilst working in the dried fruits. Divide the dough into twelve pieces and shape into buns, placing them on a floured baking sheet, quite close together, so that the buns will grow together during proving. Cover with a damp tea-towel or plastic wrap and leave by the Aga for a further 45–60 minutes, until well risen.

4 Mix together the ingredients for the paste, beating them until smooth. Spoon into a large piping bag fitted with a 4mm straight pipe. Carefully score crosses on the buns with a sharp knife, then pipe the paste over the score marks, cutting it cleanly from the end of the pipe with a sharp knife.

5 Bake the buns in the Roasting Oven for 15 minutes, then slip in the cold shelf and cook for a further 10–15 minutes.

6 Prepare the glaze while the buns are baking. Leave the ingredients in a pan on the back of the Aga for 15 minutes, then stir and bring rapidly to a boil, continuing to cook quickly for 2 minutes to make a

Makes 12

15g fresh yeast
150ml/⅔ cup warm milk
350g/2½ cups strong
    white flour
150g/1 cup wholewheat flour
½ tsp salt
½ freshly grated nutmeg
1 tsp ground cinnamon
1 tsp mixed spice
75g butter
50g/⅓ cup caster sugar
1 large egg, beaten
75g/½ cup sultanas
50g/⅓ cup currants
50g/⅓ cup mixed peel

Paste:

50g butter
150g/1 cup plain flour
100ml/½ cup warm water

Glaze:

3 tbsp caster sugar
3 tbsp milk
3 tbsp water

Aga equipment:

wire shelf on fourth set of
    runners in Roasting Oven
    with cold shelf on first or
    second set of runners
    (depending on the rise of
    your buns)

thick paste. Brush the mixture over the hot cross buns as soon as they come out of the oven.

7 Cool on a wire rack. I always prefer to serve these buns toasted, no matter how fresh they are, but you will have to toast them in the Aga toaster with the lid up on the Boiling Plate.

Chocolate Brownies

Brownies were one of our best sellers when we owned a deli – we stocked over fifty varieties of cheese, countless cold meats, gourmet coffees but it was the sales of these sticky, rich cakes that eclipsed them all!

Makes 16–20 pieces

300g good quality plain chocolate, broken into small pieces
4 tbsp golden syrup
175g unsalted butter, cut into small pieces
1 tsp natural vanilla extract or ½ tsp vanilla essence
3 large eggs, beaten
175g/1¼ cups caster sugar
125g/¾ cup plain flour
pinch of salt

Aga equipment:

small roasting tin, lined, on third set of runners in Roasting Oven, with cold shelf on second set of runners OR second set of runners in Baking Oven of four-oven Aga

1 Line the roasting tin. Melt the chocolate in a heavy-based pan on the Simmering Plate, stirring frequently – *do not allow it to catch and burn*.

2 Leave the chocolate to cool slightly, then stir in the golden syrup, butter and vanilla extract. Continue beating until the mixture is completely smooth, then beat in the eggs. Finally stir in the sugar, flour and salt, mixing thoroughly to give a thick batter.

3 Pour the batter into the prepared tin, then bake for 25–30 minutes until set.

4 Allow the brownies to cool slightly, then mark them into squares. Transfer to a wire rack, using the lining paper to lift the cakes, and leave to cool completely.

Wholewheat Sandwich Loaves

I have already explained that we make all our own bread, and the Aga cooks in much the same way as a conventional bread oven. Nick and I often run bread making courses and have been amazed at the number of Aga owners who have had trouble with traditional loaves – inserting the cold shelf half way through cooking gives a perfect result. If you have never made bread before, this is an excellent recipe to use for starters. Any flour for bread making should have a protein content of over 10 per cent – 12–14 per cent is ideal.

1 Crumble the yeast into the water in a large mixing bowl then leave for 2–3 minutes. Stir well to ensure that the yeast has dissolved, then gradually add 500g/4 cups of the wholewheat flour to give a smooth, creamy liquid. Cover the bowl and leave it by the side of the Aga for 20 minutes, until the mixture is starting to bubble.

2 Add the salt and oil, then gradually stir in the remaining wholewheat flour and the strong white flour. There is really no need to measure them accurately – just add them by the scoop or ladleful until the dough feels right. Start to bring the dough together with your hands, then turn it out on to a work surface and knead thoroughly into a soft, smooth dough. It shouldn't be sticky, so add a little extra flour if necessary during kneading. *The advantage of adding flour to water, rather than the other way round, is that you can actually judge the texture of the dough as you finish mixing it.*

3 Knead the dough by stretching it, using the heel of your hand, and then pulling it back towards you. When the dough is well developed and ready to prove, you should be able to pull an ear of it out to about 5cm. Return the dough to the bowl, then cover and leave by the side of the Aga for about an hour, until well risen and doubled in size.

4 Scrape the dough back on to the worktop and knead it lightly into shape. Divide it into two, then shape into round loaves on a baking sheet, or loaves to fit 1kg loaf tins – the dough should occupy about two-thirds of the tins. Cover with plastic wrap or a damp tea towel, and

Makes 2 large loaves

25g fresh yeast
900ml/4 cups tepid water
750g/6 cups wholewheat
  bread flour
1 tbsp salt
2 tbsp fruity olive oil
300g/3 cups strong
  white flour

Aga equipment:

wire shelf on floor in Roasting
  Oven then cold shelf on
  first or second set of
  runners

leave by the side of the Aga for a further 30 minutes, until well risen – *the dough should rise quite proud of the loaf tins, if you are using them.*

5 Remove the covering and scatter a little extra flour over the loaves, if you wish. Bake on the wire shelf on the floor of the Roasting Oven for 25 minutes, then insert the cold shelf on the first or second set of runners depending on the rise of your loaf. Continue to bake for a further 20 minutes. Shake the loaves out of the tins (loosen them with a knife if necessary) or loosen them from the baking sheet. Tap the bottom of the loaves – they should sound hollow if cooked. If not, return them to the wire shelf without their tins and cook for a further 5 minutes. Resist temptation and allow the bread to cool on a wire rack.

Wholewheat Oatmeal Olive Oil Loaf

A nutty, rustic loaf with a coarse texture of oatmeal. I like to soak the oatmeal before adding it to the mix, which softens it slightly. Although I usually advocate fresh yeast as I think it makes a better loaf, I have used the easy-blend variety here for a quick bread requiring only one rising.

Makes 1 loaf

150g/1 cup medium oatmeal
250ml/1 cup tepid water
125g/1 cup wholewheat flour
100g/1 cup strong white flour
2 tsp salt
1 sachet easy-blend yeast
5 tbsp/⅓ cup fruity olive oil
75–100ml/⅓–½ cup tepid water
olive oil for proving

Toppings:

1 tsp coarse salt
1 tsp fresh rosemary
1 large clove garlic, finely sliced

1 Soak the oatmeal in the tepid water for about 20 minutes, until completely soft – stand the bowl on the back of the Aga to keep the ingredients warm.

2 Add the remaining ingredients, then turn the mixture on to a floured surface and knead thoroughly, and shape into a flat, round loaf about 20cm in diameter. *Don't expect this mixture to become as stretchy as an ordinary dough.* Drizzle a little olive oil into a tray and place the loaf in the oil to prove. Cover it with plastic wrap or a clean, damp tea-towel and leave by the Aga for about 1 hour, until well risen.

3 Carefully turn the loaf over on to the floor of the Roasting Oven. Sprinkle with the toppings, then bake for 20 minutes. Allow the bread to cool on a wire rack before eating. This is an excellent loaf to serve with soup.

Naan Breads

I use the floor of the Roasting Oven like a tandoor – a traditional Indian clay oven – to cook these flat breads. When shaping the naans, experiment with adding fillings such as chopped garlic and coriander, or coconut and sultanas.

1 Crumble the yeast into the warm milk and leave to stand for 2–3 minutes before whisking to ensure that it is completely dissolved.

2 Mix the flour, salt and sugar together in a large bowl and make a well in the centre. Tip in the yeast, egg and 3 tablespoons of the yogurt, then mix to a soft, manageable dough, adding a little extra milk if necessary. Turn the dough on to the work surface and knead thoroughly until soft, smooth and stretchy. Return the dough to the bowl, then cover and leave it by the side of the Aga until it has doubled in size.

3 Scrape the dough back on to the work surface and divide it into six, shaping into balls whilst kneading lightly. This is when you would add a filling. Cover and leave to rest for about 10 minutes, until slightly puffy.

4 Roll and pull each piece of dough into a large tear-drop shape about 20cm in length. Brush the naans with the remaining yogurt then bake them immediately, three at a time, on the floor of the Roasting Oven for 5–8 minutes, until slightly puffed and cooked. Flip the breads over for just a few seconds to lightly colour (not brown) the tops. Spread with a little butter before serving – keep the first batch warm in a clean tea-towel or napkin in the Simmering Oven while cooking the remaining breads.

Makes 6

15g fresh yeast
50ml/¼ cup warm milk
500g/3½ cups plain flour
1 tsp salt
1 tsp caster sugar
1 large egg
150g natural yogurt or
   buttermilk
50g butter, melted and
   cooled

Roasted Garlic & Sage Foccacia

A foccacia is a flat Italian bread, often drenched in olive oil and usually with coarse sea salt pressed into the top. I love experimenting with different flavourings and this is one of my favourite combinations.

Makes 1 large loaf

15g fresh yeast
250ml/1 cup warm water
500g/3½ cups strong white flour
2 tsp salt
1–2 tbsp sage, freshly chopped, or 1 tsp dried
5 tbsp/⅓ cup fruity olive oil
6 large juicy garlic cloves
olive oil
1 tbsp ground rice
coarse salt for baking

Aga equipment:

wire shelf on third set of runners in Roasting Oven

1 Crumble the yeast into the warm water and leave to stand for a few minutes. Mix together the flour, salt and sage in a large bowl, then whisk the yeast liquid and add it to the bowl with the olive oil. Mix into a soft, manageable dough, adding a little more warm water if necessary, then knead thoroughly until smooth and pliable. Return the dough to the bowl, cover with a damp tea-towel or plastic wrap and leave near the Aga for 1 hour, until doubled in size.

2 Meanwhile, place the unpeeled garlic in a small tin, drizzle with a little olive oil and roast on the shelf in the Roasting Oven for 15–20 minutes. Allow to cool, then scoop the soft garlic out of the skins and chop it roughly. Remove the shelf from the oven.

3 Knock the dough back lightly, incorporating the garlic as you knead. Stretch or roll the dough into a flat, oval loaf about 30x20cm. Drizzle 1–2 tablespoons of olive oil on to a tray, then place the loaf in the oil, smoothest side down. Cover with the damp towel or fresh plastic wrap and leave by the Aga for a further 30–40 minutes, until well risen. *The dough will absorb most of the oil during this rising.*

4 Sprinkle the loaf with the ground rice – the side you are looking at now will be the base, so the rice will give an extra crispy crust during baking. Scoop up the dough carefully, turning it over and placing it gently on the floor of the Roasting Oven. Scatter a little coarse salt over the dough and bake for 20–25 minutes, then allow the loaf to cool slightly before serving. The loaf may be baked in a square, shallow tin on the wire shelf on the floor of the oven, if preferred.

Hazelnut & Raisin Rolls

An unusual bread which is good for dinner parties, being just that little bit different. Try serving it with Moorish Humus (page 19) – an excellent combination.

1 Crumble the yeast into half the water, then leave it to stand for 2–3 minutes. Mix the flours and salt together in a large mixing bowl, make a well in the centre and add the olive oil. Whisk the yeast liquid, to ensure that the yeast has properly dissolved, then add it to the bowl with half the remaining water.

2 Mix to a soft but manageable dough, adding as much of the remaining water as necessary. Turn out on to a floured surface and knead thoroughly until the dough is smooth and elastic. Return the dough to the bowl, cover it with plastic wrap or a damp tea towel and leave it by the Aga for about an hour, until well risen and almost doubled in size.

3 Scrape the risen dough on to the work surface, then knead it gently, incorporating the nuts and raisins. Divide the dough into twelve pieces then shape into rolls. Place them on a floured baking sheet, cover and leave by the Aga for a further 30 minutes until puffy and well-risen.

4 Bake the rolls for 15 minutes, then insert the cold shelf and bake for a further 5–10 minutes. Cool the rolls for 15–20 minutes, then serve them warm. Alternatively, warm the rolls for 10–15 minutes in a basket in the Simmering Oven.

Makes 12

15g fresh yeast
450ml/2 cups tepid water
300g/3 cups wholewheat flour
200g/1¾ cups strong white flour
2 tsp salt
2 tbsp olive oil
75g hazelnuts, roughly chopped
50g/⅓ cup seedless raisins, roughly chopped

Aga equipment:

wire shelf on fourth set of runners in Roasting Oven with cold shelf on second set of runners

Pain Rustique

A light, French-style loaf which takes a little longer to prepare than many breads as the dough actually has three risings. A clean, tightly folded tea-towel is wrapped around the loaf for the final rising, to create a tight, upright bread.

Makes 1 loaf

15g fresh yeast
350ml/1½ cups tepid water
500g/3½ cups strong
white flour
125g/1 cup wholewheat flour
1 tbsp salt
ground rice for baking

Aga equipment:

wire rack on floor of
Roasting Oven

1 Crumble the yeast into the warm liquid and leave for 3–4 minutes, then stir until completely dissolved. Mix together the flours and salt in a large bowl, make a well in the centre and pour in the yeast liquid. Mix to a firm, manageable dough, adding just a little extra water if necessary.

2 Turn the dough out on to a lightly floured work surface and knead thoroughly until the dough is really smooth and elastic in texture, then return it to the mixing bowl and cover with a damp cloth or plastic wrap. Leave the bowl by the side of the Aga for about an hour, until the dough has doubled in size.

3 Scrape the dough out of the bowl and re-knead it, but more lightly than the first time. Replace it in the bowl, cover and leave by the side of the Aga for a further 30 minutes, until it has risen again.

4 Lightly oil a baking sheet and scatter ground rice in a circle about 15–17.5cm in diameter in the centre. Knock back the dough and shape it into a perfectly round loaf, then place it on top of the ground rice. Tightly fold a clean tea towel on the bias and wrap it firmly around the sides of the loaf, to force it to rise upwards and keep its shape. Cover loosely with plastic wrap and leave by the side of the Aga for a further 45 minutes, or until doubled in size. This is the third rising.

5 Holding the dough steady with the tea-towel, make three deep slashes across the top of the loaf, then remove the towel. Bake the loaf on the wire rack for 30–35 minutes, until the base sounds hollow when tapped. Cool on a wire rack.

Ciabatta

Use ciabatta flour for this Italian bread if possible, as it will stretch more readily than other flours to give the characteristic open or 'holey' texture. Larger supermarkets and health food shops should have it in their speciality flour range. Ciabattas need an overnight starter, and are easiest to mix in a table mixer, not a food processor.

1 Crumble the yeast for the starter into the warm water, leave to soften for 1–2 minutes, then stir until completely dissolved. Add the flour and stir until the ingredients are just mixed together, then cover and leave close to the Aga overnight, or for 12 hours.

2 Crumble the remaining yeast into the warm milk in the bowl of your mixer. Leave it to soften, then stir until completely dissolved. Add the water, oil and the starter and mix with the beater until blended – the starter will be sticky so mix thoroughly. Add the flour and salt and mix for 2–3 minutes before changing the beater for the dough hook. Knead for 2 minutes at low speed, followed by 2 minutes at a medium speed.

3 Turn the dough out on to a floured surface and knead lightly by hand – only add enough flour to make the dough manageable as too much will change the texture of the bread. Return the dough to the bowl, cover and leave by the side of the Aga for about 1 hour, until doubled in size and full of air bubbles.

4 Scrape the dough out on to a well floured surface – divide it into four pieces but do not knock it back. Roll the pieces into loaf shapes then press them flat, pulling them into slipper shapes about 25x10cm. Pour a thin layer of olive oil over the base of a tray large enough to take the four loaves, then place the loaves on the tray, smoothest side downwards, so that the dough will become coated in the oil during the next rising. Dimple the doughs firmly with your fingers – this prevents them from rising too much. Cover with damp cloths and leave for 1–1½ hours by the side of the Aga. The loaves will become puffy but should not rise dramatically.

5 Baking the loaves requires a flick of the wrist! Scatter the ground rice over the puffy dough – if it has really risen, dimple the dough

Makes 4 loaves

10g yeast
5 tbsp/⅓ cup warm milk
250ml/1 cup warm water
2 tbsp fruity olive oil
450g/3 cups ciabatta flour
  or plain flour
1 tbsp salt
extra olive oil for baking
2 tbsp ground rice

Starter:

10g fresh yeast
250ml/1 cup warm water
300g/2 cups ciabatta flour
  or plain flour

again gently before adding the rice. Carefully turn the loaves over, twisting them slightly and scooping up a little of the oil with each piece. Pull them gently to maintain the slipper shape, and place them on the floor of the Roasting Oven – you should be able to fit all four in at once, but bake the loaves in two batches if you prefer. Try not throw the loaves down or the air will be knocked out of the bread.

6 Bake the ciabattas for about 15 minutes, until the bases are browned and crisp and the tops are firm but still pale in colour. Moisten the loaves with a fine water spray once or twice during baking – this helps to prevent browning. Cool briefly on a wire rack before slicing and eating warm.

Chapattis

These are one of the easiest Indian breads to make and should be cooked directly on the Simmering Plate of the Aga.

Makes 12

1 tbsp butter or ghee
325g/3 cups fine wholewheat flour or gram/chapatti flour
½ tsp salt
250ml/1 cup warm water (approximately)
1 tbsp extra flour in a shallow bowl or plate

1 Rub the butter or ghee into the flour and salt, then add sufficient water to form a soft dough – the amount of water required will depend on the texture of the flour. Knead the dough until smooth on a floured surface, then cover and leave for 30 minutes.

2 Divide the dough into twelve pieces then roll each piece into a ball between the palms of your hands. Flatten, then dip each one into the extra flour. Roll into circles about 9cm/6 inches in diameter. Cook the chapattis directly on the Simmering Plate for 30 seconds on each side, until brown spots appear. Keep the chapattis warm in a piece of aluminium foil lined with absorbent kitchen paper until all the breads are cooked.

Morning Rolls

What better way to impress your overnight guests than by offering fresh bread from your Aga for breakfast? For an 8am breakfast you will need to be up about 6am – but you can go back to bed after kneading and shaping the rolls. It really is worth it!

1 Crumble the yeast into the water for the overnight dough, soften for 1–2 minutes then stir until dissolved. Mix the flour and salt in a large bowl and add the yeast liquid. Stir just until the ingredients are combined, then cover the bowl and leave it by the side of the Aga overnight.

2 In the morning, add the remaining ingredients, crumbling the yeast in the water as before, and adding the flour gradually until you have a workable dough. Knead thoroughly on a lightly floured surface until the dough is smooth and pliable.

3 Divide the dough immediately into 18 pieces. Shape into smooth round rolls and place them on floured baking sheets, then cover with clean damp cloths and leave to rise for about 30 minutes by the Aga. The rolls should be quite close together, so that they will grow into each other and break apart when cooked – I usually fit 15 on to a Swiss roll tin.

4 Bake the rolls for 20 minutes with the cold shelf in position. They should be golden brown but still soft and not too crusty. Cool on a wire rack for at least 10 minutes before serving.

Makes 18 rolls

Overnight dough:

25g yeast
450ml/2 cups water
450g/3 cups strong
   white flour
15g salt

Morning dough:

25g yeast
175ml/¾ cup warm water
450g/3 cups strong white
   flour (approximately)
50g butter, cut into small
   pieces
1 tbsp caster sugar

Aga equipment:

wire shelf on third set of
   runners in Roasting Oven
   with cold shelf on top set
   of runners

Weights & Measures

Metrication is an inevitability in the UK – most of our groceries are sold in metric packs – and these only state the metric weight – so it doesn't really make sense to continue quoting pounds and ounces in recipes. It really is quite easy to think in grams but it is imperative to take a sensible approach to weighing ingredients, to keep things as accurate as possible.

The Guild of Food Writers metrication chart, which I use for reference, has adopted a gram-friendly policy – it takes convenient metric weights and gives the UK equivalent in a less user-friendly amount. Thus it is better to use quantities such as 50g, 100g and 125g than, for example, using 90g as a conversion for 3oz, which would be virtually impossible to weigh accurately.

Agas are now becoming very popular in America, where the standard measure for ingredients is cups. I have included a lot of cup measures in the recipes, but you will need to consult the chart above for weights of ingredients such as butter, which are stated only in grams.

Spoon sizes

Metric spoon sizes are 15ml, 10ml and 5ml. As these are so close to existing spoon sizes, and in line with European practice, The Guild of Food Writers recommends the continued use of tablespoons, dessertspoons and teaspoons.

WEIGHT/SOLIDS		VOLUME/LIQUIDS	
15g	½oz	15ml	½fl oz
25g	1oz	30ml	1fl oz
40g	1½oz	50ml	2fl oz
50g	1¾oz	100ml	3½fl oz
75g	2¾oz	125ml	4fl oz
100g	3½oz	150ml	5fl oz (¼ pint)
125g	4½oz	200ml	7fl oz (⅓ pint)
150g	5½oz	250ml (¼ litre)	9fl oz
175g	6oz	300ml	10fl oz (½ pint)
200g	7oz	350ml	12fl oz
225g	8oz	400ml	14fl oz
250g	9oz	425ml	15fl oz (¾ pint)
275g	9½oz	450ml	16fl oz
300g	10½oz	500ml (½ litre)	18fl oz
325g	11½oz	600ml	1 pint (20fl oz)
350g	12oz	700ml	1¼ pints
400g	14oz	850ml	1½ pints
425g	15oz	1litre	1¾ pints
450g	1lb	1.2 litres	2 pints
500g	1lb 2oz	1.5 litres	2¾ pints
600g	1lb 5oz	2 litres	3½ pints
700g	1lb 9oz	2.5 litres	4½ pints
750g	1lb 10oz	3 litres	5¼ pints
1kg	2lb 4oz		
1.25kg	2lb 12oz		
1.5kg	3lb 5oz		
2kg	4lb 8oz		
2.25kg	5lb		
2.5kg	5lb 8oz		
3kg	6lb 8oz		

Further Reading

THE AGA BOOK by Mary Berry (published by Aga) is an essential Aga reference, containing many basic facts, cooking charts etc.

Useful Mail Order Addresses

Most of us nowadays have access to a large supermarket. However, some of us live in the country and are not able to pop out to collect the odd ingredient that will make a dish. Others will be in huge conurbations with every conceivable type of ethnic grocer to hand, as well as major food halls and superstores.

Those with a goodly-sized vegetable patch may like to grow some of the more unusual vegetables and salads that are now commonplace in contemporary cuisine. Those far from a good fishmonger may appreciate a mail order fresh fish company and others may just like access to some of my favourite suppliers. I hope that these addresses will be useful:

HERBS, SPICES AND SEASONINGS
A huge selection in sensible quantities:
Foxes Spices, Masons Road,
Stratford-Upon-Avon CV37 9NF
Tel: (01789) 266420 Fax: (01789) 267737

Seasoned Pioneers, 101 Summers Road,
Brunswick Business Park, Liverpool, L3 4BJ
Freephone: (0800) 068 2348
Tel/Fax: (0151) 709 9330
Email: info@seasonedpioneers.co.uk
Website: www.seasonedpioneers.co.uk

VEGETABLE AND HERB SEEDS SUPPLIERS
(including rare varieties):
S.E. Marshall & Co Ltd, Wisbech,
Cambs PE13 2RF
Tel: (01945) 583407 Fax: (01945) 588235
Website: www.marshalls-seeds.co.uk

Suffolk Herbs, Monks Farm, Pantlings Lane,
Kelvedon, Essex CO5 9PG
Tel: (01376) 572456 Fax: (01376) 571189

An organisation to join and support (includes the Heritage Seed Programme):
The Henry Doubleday Research Association
(a registered charity)
Ryton Organic Gardens, Coventry CV8 3LG
Tel: (02476) 303517 Fax: (02476) 639229
Email: enquiry@hdra.org.uk
Website: www.hdra.org.uk

ITALIAN SPECIALITIES
Lavish Christmas mail order catalogue, basics available by mail order all year:
Carluccios,
28A Neal Street, London WC2H 9PS
Tel: 0207-580 3050 Fax: 0207-580 3070
Email: carluccios@cix.compulink.co.uk
Website: www.carluccios.com

SPECIALIST FLOURS FOR BREAD MAKING
Superb stone ground and specialist flours, including ciabatta flour:
Shipton Mill Limited, Long Newnton,
Tetbury, Gloucestershire GL8 8RP
Tel: (01666) 505050 Fax: (01666) 504666

COFFEE
Delicious coffees, freshly roasted before despatch. teas and gourmet drinking chocolate:
Torz & Macatonia, Unit 12, Blackwall Trading
Estate, Lanrick Road, London E14 0JP
Tel: (0171) 515 7770 Fax: (0171) 515 7779

Index

151